Love Poems

Love Poems

Edited by Johanna Brownell

CASTLE BOOKS

For B.R.S.

With love

This edition published by
CASTLE BOOKS
a division of Book Sales, Inc.
114 Northfield Avenue
Edison, NJ 08837

Designed by Tony Meisel
Printed in the United States of America

ISBN 0-7858-1332-2

Contents

Intoduction

Poetry, by its very nature, is one of the most personal and emotional of literary art forms. The ability to tell a story, evoke a mood or express an emotion within the confines of several lines or pages is a difficult and challenging enterprise. Furthermore, the poet must draw us into his world, open his heart and mind and, through a deliberate choice of words, evoke both meaning and feeling so as to encourage us to open ours. This is especially true of love poetry. The stories, feelings and emotions the poet shares through his verse are especially personal in nature and require understanding and compassion, if not similar experiences, in order to be fully appreciated. Thus, when reading and selecting the poems for this book, I found myself bound by my own personal preferences and experiences. Still, I did attempt to collect a wide variety of poems that reflect the different faces and feelings of love, as well as that represent English language love poetry from the mid-16th century to the beginning of the 20th century. Moreover, I endeavored to include the beautiful works of many lesser-known poets. In the end, I was left with a wealth of emotion and feeling, as well as with a firm belief that, although language may change and evolve, the expression of love remains a constant throughout time.

NICHOLAS BRETON
(ca. 1545–1626)

An Odd Conceit

LOVELY kind, and kindly loving,
Such a mind were worth the moving:
Truly fair, and fairly true, –
Where are all these, but in you?

Wisely kind, and kindly wise;
Blessed life, where such love lies!
Wise, and kind, and fair, and true, –
Lovely live all these in you.

Sweetly dear, and dearly sweet;
Blessed, where these blessings meet!
Sweet, fair, wise, kind, blessed, true, –
Blessed be all these in you!

Sonnet

PRETTY twinkling starry eyes,
How did nature first devise
Such a sparkling in your sight
As to give Love such delight
As to make him, like a fly,
Play with looks until he die?

Sure you were not made at first
For such mischief to be cursed:
As to kill affection's care,
That doth only truth declare!
Where worth's wonders never wither
Love and beauty live together.

Blessed eyes, then give your blessing,
That, in passion's best expressing,
Love, that only lives to grace ye,
May not suffer to deface ye,
But in gentle thoughts directions,
Show the praise of your perfections.

EDMUND SPENSER
(ca. 1552–1599)

One Day I Wrote Her Name

ONE day I wrote her name upon the strand,
    But came the waves and washed it away:
    Again I wrote it with a second hand,
    But came the tide, and made my pains his prey.
Vain man, said she, that dost in vain essay
    A mortal thing so to immortalize,
    For I myself shall like to this decay,
    And eke my name be wiped out likewise.
Not so (quoth I) let baser things devise
    To die in dust, but you shall live by fame:
    My verse your virtues rare shall eternize,
    And in the heavens write your glorious name.
Whereas whenas death shall all the world subdue,
    Our love shall live, and later life renew.

Sovereign Beauty

THE sovereign beauty which I do admire,
  Witness the world how worthy to be praised:
  The light whereof hath kindled heavenly fire
  In my frail spirit by her from baseness raised,
That being now with her huge brightness dazed,
  Base thing I can no more endure to view:
  But looking still on her I stand amazed
  At wondrous sight of so celestial hue.
So when my tongue would speak her praises due,
  It stopped is with thought's astonishment:
  And when my pen would write her titles true,
  It ravished is with fancy's wonderment:
Yet in my heart I then both speak and write
  The wonder that my wit cannot endite.

Most Happy Letters

MOST happy letters, fram'd by skilful trade,
    With which that happy name was first design'd:
    The which three times thrice happy hath me made,
    With gifts of body, fortune, and of mind.
The first my being to me gave by kind,
    From mother's womb deriv'd by due descent,
    The second is my sovereign Queen most kind,
    That honour and large richesse to me lent.
The third my love, my life's last ornament,
    By whom my spirit out of dust was raised:
    To speak her praise and glory excellent,
    Of all alive most worthy to be praised.
Ye three Elizabeths for ever live,
    That three such graces did unto me give.

SIR PHILIP SIDNEY
(1554–1586)

From "Astrophel and Stella"

I

LOVING in truth, and fain in verse my love to show,
That she, dear she might take some pleasure of my
    pain, –
Pleasure might cause her read, reading might make her
    know,
Knowledge might pity win, and pity grace obtain, –
I sought fit words to paint the blackest face of woe;
Studying inventions fine, her wits to entertain,
Oft turning others' leaves, to see if thence would flow
Some fresh and fruitful showers upon my sun-burn'd
    brain.
But words came halting forth, wanting Invention's stay;
Invention, Nature's child, fled step-dame Study's blows,
And others' feet still seem'd but strangers in my way.
Thus, great with child to speak, and helpless in my
    throes,
Biting my truant pen, beating myself for spite;
Fool, said my Muse to me, look in thy heart and
    write.

THE wisest scholar of the wight most wise
By Phoebus' doom, with sugar'd sentence says,
That Virtue, if it once met with our eyes,
Strange flames of love it in our souls would raise;
But for that man with pain his truth descries,
Whiles he each thing in sense's balance weighs,
And so nor will, nor can behold those skies
Which inward sun to heroic mind displays,
Virtue of late with virtuous care to stir
Love of herself, took Stella's shape, that she
To mortal eyes might sweetly shine in her.
It is most true, for since I her did see,
Virtue's great beauty in that face I prove,
And find th'effect, for I do burn in love.

SAMUEL DANIEL
(1562-1619)

From "Delia"

I

UNTO the boundless ocean of thy beauty
    Runs this poor river, charged with streams of zeal,
    Returning thee the tribute of my duty,
    Which here my love, my youth, my plaints reveal.
Here I unclasp the book of my charged soul,
    Where I have cast th'accounts of all my care:
    Here have I summed my sighs. Here I enrol
    How they were spent for thee. Look what they are.
Look on the dear expences of my youth,
    And see how just I reckon with thine eyes.
    Examine well they beauty in my truth,
    And cross my cares ere greater sums arise.
Read it, sweet maid, though it be done but slightly;
Who can show all his love, doth love but lightly.

II

GO, wailing verse, the infants of my love,
　　Minerva-like, brought forth without a mother,
　　Present the image of the cares I prove;
　　Witness your father's grief exceeds all other.
Sigh out a story of her cruel deeds,
　　With interrupted accents of despair:
　　A monument that whosoever reads
　　May justly praise, and blame my loveless Fair.
Say her disdain hath dried up my blood,
　　And starved you, in succours still denying;
　　Press to her eyes, importune me some good;
　　Waken her sleeping pity with your crying.
Knock at that hard heart, beg till you have moved her,
And tell th'unkind how dearly I have loved her.

XXXVIII

WHEN men shall find thy flower, thy glory pass,
    And thou with carefull brow sitting alone
    Received hast this message from thy glass
    That tells thee truth, and says that all is gone;
Fresh shalt thou see in me the wounds thou mad'st;
    Though spent thy flame, in me the heat remaining.
    I that have loved thee thus before thou fad'st,
    My faith shall wax, when thou art in thy waning.
The world shall find this miracle in me,
    That fire can burn, when all the matter's spent;
    Then what my faith hath been thy self shalt see,
    And that thou wast unkind thou mayst repent.
Thou mayst repent, that thou hast scorned my tears,
When winter snows upon thy sable hairs.

XLIII

MOST fair and lovely maid, look from the shore,
    See thy Leander striving in these waves,
    Poor soul forespent, whose force can do no more.
    Now send forth hopes, for now calm pity saves,
And waft him to thee with those lovely eyes,
    A happy convoy to a holy land.
    Now show thy power and where thy virtue lies;
    To save thine own, stretch out the fairest hand.
Stretch out the fairest hand a pledge of peace,
    That hand that darts so right and never misses;
    I shall forget old wrongs; my griefs shall cease;
    For that which gave me wounds, I'll give it kisses.
Once let the ocean of my cares find shore,
That thou be pleased, and I may sigh no more.

WILLIAM SHAKESPEARE
(1564–1616)

Sonnet 15

WHEN I consider everything that grows
Holds in perfection but a little moment,
That this huge stage presenteth naught but shows
Whereon the stars in secret influence comment;
When I perceive that men as plants increase,
Cheered and checked even by the selfsame sky,
Vaunt in their youthful sap, at height decrease,
And wear their brave state out of memory;
Then the conceit of this inconstant stay
Sets you most rich in youth before my sight,
Where wasteful Time debateth with Decay
To change your day of youth to sullied night;
    And all in war with Time for love of you,
    As he takes from you, I engraft you new.

Sonnet 18

SHALL I compare thee to a summer's day?
Thou art more lovely and more temperate:
Rough winds do shake the darling buds of May,
And summer's lease hath all too short a date:
Sometime too hot the eye of heaven shines,
And often is his gold complexion dimmed;
And every fair from fair sometime declines,
By chance, or nature's changing course untrimmed;
But thy eternal summer shall not fade,
Nor lose possession of that fair thou ow'st,
Nor shall death brag thou wander'st in his shade,
When in eternal lines to time thou grow'st;
    So long as men can breathe, or eyes can see,
    So long lives this, and this gives life to thee.

Sonnet 25

LET those who are in favour with their stars
Of public honour and proud titles boast,
Whilst I, whom fortune of such triumph bars,
Unlook'd for joy in that I honour most.
Great princes' favourites their fair leaves spread
But as the marigold at the sun's eye,
And in themselves their pride lies buried,
For at a frown they in their glory die.
The painful warrior famoused for fight,
After a thousand victories once foiled,
Is from the book of honour rased quite,
And all the rest forgot for which he toiled:
    Then happy I, that love and am beloved
    Where I may not remove nor be removed.

Sonnet 53

WHAT is your substance, whereof are you made,
That millions of strange shadows on you tend?
Since everyone hath, every one, one shade,
And you, but one, can every shadow lend.
Describe Adonis, and the counterfeit
Is poorly imitated after you;
On Helen's cheek all art of beauty set,
And you in Grecian tires are painted new.
Speak of the spring and foison of the year,
The one doth shadow of your beauty show,
The other as your bounty doth appear,
And you in every blessed shape we know.
    In all external grace you have some part,
      But you like none, none you, for constant heart.

Sonnet 73

THAT time of year thou mayst in me behold
When yellow leaves, or none, or few, do hang
Upon those boughs which shake against the cold,
Bare ruined choirs, where late the sweet birds sang.
In me thou see'st the twilight of such day
As after sunset fadeth in the west,
Which by and by black night doth take away,
Death's second self, that seals up all in rest.
In me thou see'st the glowing of such fire
That on the ashes of his youth doth lie,
As the death-bed whereon it must expire,
Consum'd with that which it was nourish'd by.
   This thou perceivest, which makes thy love more
   strong,
   To love that well which thou must leave ere long.

Sonnet 104

TO me, fair Friend, you never can be old,
For as you were when first your eye I eyed
Such seems your beauty still. Three winters cold
Have from the forests shook three summers' pride;
Three beauteous springs to yellow autumn turned
In process of the seasons have I seen,
Three April perfumes in three hot Junes burned,
Since first I saw you fresh, which yet are green.
Ah! yet doth beauty, like a dial-hand,
Steal from his figure, and no pace perceived;
So your sweet hue, which methinks still doth stand,
Hath motion, and mine eye may be deceived:
    For fear of which, hear this, thou age unbred:
    Ere you were born, was beauty's summer dead.

Sonnet 105

LET not my love be called idolatry
Nor my beloved as an idol show,
Since all alike my songs and praises be
To one, of one, still such, and ever so.
Kind is my love to-day, to-morrow kind,
Still constant in a wondrous excellence;
Therefore my verse, to constancy confined,
One thing expressing, leaves out difference.
Fair, kind, and true is all my argument,
Fair, kind, and true, varying to other words;
And in this change is my invention spent,
Three themes in one, which wondrous scope affords.
 Fair, kind, and true have often lived alone,
 Which three till now never kept seat in one.

Sonnet 116

LET me not to the marriage of true minds
Admit impediments. Love is not love
Which alters when it alteration finds,
Or bends with the remover to remove.
O, no! it is an ever-fixed mark,
That looks on tempests and is never shaken;
It is the star to every wandering bark,
Whose worth's unknown, although his height be taken.
Love 's not Time's fool, though rosy lips and cheeks
Within his bending sickle's compass come;
Love alters not with his brief hours and weeks,
But bears it out even to the edge of doom.
    If this be error, and upon me proved,
    I never writ, nor no man ever loved.

Sonnet 130

MY mistress' eyes are nothing like the sun
Coral is far more red than her lips' red:
If snow be white, why then her breasts are dun;
If hairs be wires, black wires grow on her head.
I have seen roses damasked, red and white,
But no such roses see I in her cheeks;
And in some perfumes is there more delight
Than in the breath that from my mistress reeks.
I love to hear her speak, yet well I know
That music hath a far more pleasing sound:
I grant I never saw a goddess go,—
My mistress, when she walks, treads on the ground.
 And yet, by heaven, I think my love as rare
 As any she belied with false compare.

Sonnet 148

O ME! what eyes hath Love put in my head
Which have no correspondence with true sight!
Or if they have, where is my judgment fled
That censures falsely what they see aright?
If that be fair whereon my false eyes dote,
What means the world to say it is not so?
If it be not, then Love doth well denote
Love's eye is not so true as all men's No,
How can it? O how can Love's eye be true,
That is so vexed with watching and with tears?
No marvel then though I mistake my view:
The sun itself sees not till heaven clears.
    O cunning Love! with tears thou keep'st me blind,
    Lest eyes well-seeing thy foul faults should find!

Sonnet 152

IN loving thee thou know'st I am forsworn
But thou art twice forsworn, to me love swearing;
In act thy bed-vow broke, and new faith torn,
In vowing new hate after new love bearing.
But why of two oaths' breach do I accuse thee,
When I break twenty? I am perjur'd most;
For all my vows are oaths but to misuse thee,
And all my honest faith in thee is lost;
For I have sworn deep oaths of thy deep kindness,
Oaths of thy love, thy truth, thy constancy;
And, to enlighten thee, gave eyes to blindness,
Or made them swear against the thing they see;
    For I have sworn thee fair; more perjured I,
    To swear against the truth so foul a lie!

O Mistress Mine!
Where Are You Roaming?

(excerpt from "Twelfth Night")

O MISTRESS mine! where are you roaming?
O, stay and hear! your true love's coming,
    That can sing both high and low:
Trip no further, pretty sweeting;
Journeys end in lovers meeting,
    Every wise man's son doth know.

    What is love? 'tis not hereafter;
Present mirth hath present laughter;
    What's to come is still unsure:
In delay there lies no plenty;
Then come kiss me, sweet and twenty!
    Youth's a stuff will not endure.

Excerpt from "King Henry V"

("King Henry V", Act V, Scene 2)

King Henry V: Marry, if you would put me to verses or to dance for your sake, Kate, why you undid me: for the one, I have neither words nor measure, and for the other, I have no strength in measure, yet a reasonable measure in strength. If I could win a lady at leap-frog, or by vaulting into my saddle with my armour on my back, under the correction of bragging be it spoken, I should quickly leap into a wife. Or if I might buffet for my love, or bound my horse for her favours, I could lay on like a butcher and sit like a jack-an-apes, never off. But, before God, Kate, I cannot look greenly nor gasp out my eloquence, nor I have no cunning in protestation; only down-right oaths, which I never use till urged, nor never break for urging. If thou canst love a fellow of this temper, Kate, whose face is not worth sun-burning, that never looks in his glass for love of any thing he sees there, let thine eye be thy cook. I speak to thee plain soldier: If thou canst love me for this, take me: if not, to say to thee that I shall die, is true; but for thy love, by the Lord, no; yet I love thee too. And while thou livest, dear Kate, take a fellow of plain and uncoined constancy; for he perforce must do thee right, because he hath not the gift to woo in other places: for these fellows of infinite tongue, that can rhyme themselves into ladies' favours, they do al-ways reason themselves out again. What! A speaker is but a prater; a rhyme is but a ballad. A good leg will fall; a straight back will stoop; a black beard will turn white; a curled pate will grow bald; a fair face will wither; a full eye will wax hollow: but a good heart, Kate, is the sun and the moon; or, rather, the sun, and not the moon; for it shines bright and never changes, but keeps his course truly. If thou would have such a one, take me; and take me, take a soldier; take a soldier, take a king. And what sayest thou then to my love? speak, my fair, and fairly, I pray thee.

The Phoenix and the Turtle

LET the bird of loudest lay
On the sole Arabian tree
Herald sad and trumpet be,
To whose sound chaste wings obey.

But thou shrieking harbinger,
Foul precurser of the fiend,
Augur of the fever's end,
To this troop come thou not near.

From this session interdict
Every fowl of tyrant wing,
Save the eagle, feather'd king;
Keep the obsequy so strict.

Let the priest in surplice white,
That defunctive music can,
Be the death-divining swan,
Lest the requiem lack his right.

And thou treble-dated crow,
That thy sable gender mak'st
With the breath thou giv'st and tak'st,
'Mongst our mourners shalt thou go.

Here the anthem doth commence:
Love and constancy is dead;
Phoenix and the Turtle fled
In a mutual flame from hence.

So they lov'd, as love in twain
Had the essence but in one;
Two distincts, division none:
Number there in love was slain.

Hearts remote, yet not asunder;
Distance and no space was seen
'Twixt this Turtle and his queen:
But in them it were a wonder.

So between them love did shine
That the Turtle saw his right
Flaming in the Phoenix' sight:
Either was the other's mine.

Property was thus appalled
That the self was not the same;
Single nature's double name
Neither two nor one was called.

Reason, in itself confounded,
Saw division grow together,
To themselves yet either neither,
Simple were so well compounded;

That it cried, "How true a twain
Seemeth this concordant one!
Love has reason, reason none,
If what parts can so remain."

Whereupon it made this threne
To the Phoenix and the Dove,
Co-supremes and stars of love,
As chorus to their tragic scene:

Threnos

Beauty, truth, and rarity,
Grace in all simplicity,
Here enclos'd, in cinders lie.

Death is now the Phoenix' nest,
And the Turtle's loyal breast
To eternity doth rest,

Leaving no posterity:
'Twas not their infirmity,
It was married chastity.

Truth may seem but cannot be;
Beauty brag but 'tis not she;
Truth and beauty buried be.

To this urn let those repair
That are either true or fair;
For these dead birds sigh a prayer.

CHRISTOPHER MARLOWE
(1564-1593)

The Passionate Shepherd to His Love

COME live with me and be my Love,
And we will all the pleasures prove
That valleys, groves, hills, and fields,
Woods, or steepy mountain yields.

And we will sit upon rocks,
Seeing the shepherds feed their flocks
By shallow rivers, to whose falls
Melodious birds sing madrigals.

And I will make thee beds of roses
And a thousand fragrant posies,
A cap of flowers, and a kirtle
Embroider'd all with leaves of myrtle.

A gown made of the finest wool
Which from our pretty lambs we pull;
Fair-lined slippers for the cold,
With buckles of the purest gold;

A belt of straw and ivy buds,
With coral clasps and amber studs;
And if these pleasures may thee move,
Come live with me, and be my Love.

The shepherds's swains shall dance and sing
For thy delight each May morning:
If these delights thy mind may move,
Then live with me and be my Love.

SIR WALTER RALEIGH
(ca. 1552–1618)

The Nymph's Reply to the Shepherd

IF all the world and love were young,
And truth in every shepherd's tongue,
These pretty pleasures might me move
To live with thee and be thy Love.

Time drives the flocks from field to fold;
When rivers rage and rocks grow cold;
And Philomel becometh dumb;
The rest complains of cares to come.

The flowers do fade, and wanton fields
To wayward Winter reckoning yields;
A honey tongue, a heart of gall,
Is fancy's spring, but sorrow's fall.

Thy gowns, thy shoes, thy beds of roses,
Thy cap, thy kirtle, and thy posies,
Soon break, soon wither—soon forgotten,
In folly ripe, in reason rotten.

Thy belt of straw and ivy buds,
The coral clasps and amber studs,—
All these in me no means can move
To come to thee and be thy Love.

But could youth last and love still breed,
Had joys no date nor age no need,
Then these delights my mind might move
To live with thee and be thy Love.

The Silent Lover

i.

PASSIONS are liken'd best to floods and streams:
    The shallow murmur, but the deep are dumb;
So, when affection yields discourse, it seems
    The bottom is but shallow whence they come.
They that are rich in words, in words discover
That they are poor in that which makes a lover.

The Silent Lover
ii.

WRONG not, sweet empress of my heart,
    The merit of true passion,
With thinking that he feels no smart,
    That sues for no compassion.

Silence in love bewrays more woe
    Than words, though ne'er so witty:
A beggar that is dumb, you know,
    May challenge double pity.

Then wrong not, dearest to my heart,
    My true, though secret passion;
He smarteth most that hides his smart,
    And sues for no compassion.

As You Came From the Holy Land

AS you came from the holy land
 Of Walsinghame,
Met you not with my true love
 By the way as you came?

How shall I know your true love,
 That have met many one,
As I went to the holy land,
 That have come, that have gone?

She is neither white nor brown,
 But as the heavens fair;
There is none hath a form so divine
 In the earth or the air.

Such a one did I meet, good sir,
 Such an angelic face,
Who like a queen, like a nymph, did appear,
 By her gate, by her grace.

She hath left me here all alone,
 All alone, as unknown,
Who sometimes did me lead with herself,
 And me loved as her own.

What's the cause that she leaves you alone,
 And a new way doth take,
Who loved you once as her own,
 And her joy did you make?

I have loved her all my youth,
 But now old, as you see:
Love likes not the falling fruit
 From the withered tree.

Know that Love is a careless child,
    And forgets promise past;
He is blind, he is deaf when he list,
    And in faith never fast.

His desire is a dureless content,
    And a trustless joy;
He is won with a world of despair,
    And is lost with a toy.

Of womenkind such indeed is the love,
    Or the word love abused,
Under which many childish desires
    And conceits are excused.

But true love is a durable fire,
    In the mind ever burning,
Never sick, never old, never dead,
    From itself never turning.

JOHN DONNE
(1572–1631)

The Extasie

WHERE, like a pillow on a bed,
    A Pregnant banke swel'd up, to rest
The violets reclining head,
    Sat we two, one anothers best.
Our hands were firmely cimented
    With a fast balme, which thence did spring,
Our eye-beames twisted, and did thred
    Our eyes, upon one double string;
So to'entergraft our hands, as yet
    Was all the meanes to make us one,
And pictures in our eyes to get
    Was all our propagation.
As 'twixt two equall Armies, Fate
    Suspends uncertaine victorie,
Our soules, (which to advance their state,
    Were gone out,) hung 'twixt her, and mee.
And whil'st our soules negotiate there,
    Wee like sepulchrall statues lay;
All day, the same our postures were,
    And wee said nothing, all the day.
If any, so by love refin'd,
    That he soules language understood,
And by good love were growen all minde,
    Within convenient distance stood,
He (though he knew not which soule spake,
    Because both meant, both spake the same)
Might thence a new concoction take,
    And part farre purer then he came.
This Extasie doth unperplex
    (We said) and tell us what we love,
Wee see by this, it was not sexe,
    Wee see, we saw not what did move:
But as all severall soules containe
    Mixture of things, they know not what,
Love, these mixt soules, doth mixe againe,

And makes both one, each this and that.
A single violet transplant,
    The strength, the colour, and the size,
(All which before was poore, and scant,)
    Redoubles still, and multiplies.
When love, with one another so
    Interinanimates two soules,
That abler soule, which thence doth flow,
    Defects of lonelinesse controules.
Wee then, who are this new soule, know,
    Of what we are compos'd, and made,
For, th'Atomies of which we grow,
    Are soules, whom no change can invade.
But O alas, so long, so farre
    Our bodies why doe wee forbeare?
They are ours, though they are not wee, Wee are
    The intelligences, they the spheare.
We owe them thankes, because they thus,
    Did us, to us, at first convay,
Yeelded their forces, sense, to us,
    Nor are drosse to us, but allay.
On man heavens influence workes not so,
    But that it first imprints the ayre,
Soe soule into the soule may flow,
    Though it to body first repaire.
As our blood labours to beget
    Spirits, as like soules as it can,
Because such fingers need to knit
    That subtile knot, which makes us man:
So must pure lovers soules descend
    T'affections, and to faculties,
Which sense may reach and apprehend,
    Else a great Prince in prison lies.
To'our bodies turne wee then, that so
    Weake men on love reveal'd may looke;
Loves mysteries in soules doe grow,
    But yet the body is his booke.
And if some lover, such as wee,
    Have heard this dialogue of one,
Let him still marke us, he shall see
    Small change, when we'are to bodies gone.

Lover's Infiniteness

IF yet I have not all thy love,
Deare, I shall never have it all,
I cannot breath one other sigh, to move,
Nor can intreat one other teare to fall,
And all my treasure, which should purchase thee,
Sighs, teares, and oathes, and letters I have spent.
Yet no more can be due to mee,
Then at the bargaine made was ment,
If then thy gift of love were partiall,
That some to mee, some should to others fall,
    Deare, I shall never have Thee All.

Or if then thou gavest mee all,
All was but All, which thou hadst then;
But if in thy heart, since, there be or shall,
New love created bee, by other men,
Which have their stocks intire, and can in teares,
In sighs, in oathes, and letters outbid mee,
This new love may beget new feares,
For, this love was not vowed by thee.
And yet it was, thy gift being generall,
The ground, thy heart is mine, what ever shall
    Grow there, deare, I should have it all.

Yet I would not have all yet,
Hee that hath all can have no more,
And since my love doth every day admit
New growth, thou shouldst have new rewards in store;
Thou canst not every day give me thy heart,
If thou canst give it, then thou never gavest it:
Loves riddles are, that though thy heart depart,
It stayes at home, and thou with losing savest it:
But wee will have a way more liberall,
Then changing hearts, to joyne them, so wee shall
    Be one, and one anothers All.

The Dreame

DEARE love, for nothing lesse then thee
Would I have broke this happy dreame,
    It was a theame
For reason, much too strong for phantasie,
Therefore thou wakd'st me wisely; yet
My Dreame thou brok'st not, but continued'st it,
Thou art so truth, that thoughts of thee suffice,
To make dreames truths; and fables histories;
Enter these armes, for since thou thoughtst it best,
Not to dreame all my dreame, let's act the rest.

As lightning, or a Tapers light,
Thine eyes, and not thy noise wak'd mee;
    Yet I thought thee
(For thou lovest truth) an Angell, at first sight,
But when I saw thou sawest my heart,
And knew'st my thoughts, beyond an Angels art,
When thou knew'st what I dreamt, when thou knew'st
    when
Excesse of joy would wake me, and cam'st then,
I must confesse, it could not chuse but bee
Prophane, to thinke thee any thing but thee.

Comming and staying show'd thee, thee,
But rising makes me doubt, that now,
    Thou art not thou.
That love is weake, where feare's as strong as hee;
'Tis not all spirit, pure, and brave,
If mixture it of *Feare, Shame, Honor,* have.
Perchance as torches which must ready bee,
Men light and put out, so thou deal'st with mee,
Thou cam'st to kindle, goest to come; Then I
Will dreame that hope againe, but else would die.

Aire and Angels

TWICE or thrice had I loved thee,
Before I knew thy face or name;
So in a voice, so in a shapelesse flame,
Angells affect us oft, and worship'd bee;
    Still when, to where thou wert, I came,
Some lovely glorious nothing I did see.
      But since my soule, whose child love is,
Takes limmes of flesh, and else could nothing doe,
    More subtile then the parent is,
Love must not be, but take a body too,
      And therefore what thou wert, and who,
        I bid Love aske, and now
That it assume thy body, I allow,
And fixe it selfe in thy lip, eye, and brow.

Whilst thus to ballast love, I thought,
And so more steddily to have gone,
With wares which would sinke admiration,
I saw, I had loves pinnace overfraught,
    Ev'ry thy haire for love to worke upon
Is much too much, some fitter must be sought;
    For, nor in nothing, nor in things
Extreme, and scatt'ring bright, can love inhere;
    Then as an Angell, face, and wings
Of aire, not pure as it, yet pure doth weare,
      So thy love may be my loves spheare;
        Just such disparitie
As is twixt Aire and Angells puritie,
'Twixt womens love, and mens will ever bee.

BEN JONSON
(ca. 1572–1637)

To Celia

DRINK to me only with thine eyes,
    And I will pledge with mine;
Or leave a kiss but in the cup,
    And I'll not look for wine.
The thirst that from the soul doth rise,
    Doth ask a drink divine:
But might I of Jove's nectar sup,
    I would not change for thine.

I sent thee late a rosy wreath,
    Not so much honouring thee,
As giving it a hope, that there
    It could not wither'd be;
But thou thereon didst only breathe,
    And sent'st back to me;
Since when it grows, and smells, I swear,
    Not of itself, but thee!

Come, My Celia

COME, my Celia, let us prove
    While we may, the sports of love;
Time will not be ours forever;
    He at length our good will sever.
Spend not then his gifts in vain.
    Suns that set may rise again;
But if once we lose this light,
    'Tis with us perpetual night.
Why should we defer our joys?

Fame and rumor are but toys.
    Cannot we delude the eyes
Of a few poor household spies,
    Or his easier ears beguile,
So removed by our wile?
    'Tis no sin love's fruit to steal;
But the sweet theft to reveal.
    To be taken, to be seen,
These have crimes accounted been.

THOMAS CAREW
(ca. 1595–1640)

Lips and Eyes

IN Celia's face a question did arise
Which were more beautifull, her lips or eyes:
We (said the eyes,) send forth those poynted darts
Which pierce the hardest adamantine hearts
From us (reply'd the lips,) proceed those blisses
Which louers reape by kind words and sweet kisses.
Then wept the eyes, and from their springs did powre
Of liquid orientall pearle a shower.
Whereat the lips mou'd with delight and pleasure,
Through a sweete smile unlockt their pearlie treasure.
And bad love judge, whether did adde more grace:
Weeping or smiling pearles to Celia's face.

To My Mistris, I Burning in Love

I BURNE, and cruell you, in vaine
Hope to quench me with disdaine;
If from your eyes, those sparkles came,
That have kindled all this flame,
What bootes it me, though now you shrowde
Those fierce Comets in a cloude?
Since all the flames that I have felt,
Could your snow yet never melt,
Nor, can your snow (though you should take
Alpes into your bosome) slake
The heate of my enamour'd heart;
But with wonder learne Loves art:
No seaes of yce can coole desire,
Equall flames must quench Loves fire:
Then thinke not that my heat can dye,
Till you burne aswell as I.

The Complement

O MY deerest I shall grieve thee
When I sweare, yet sweete beleeve me,
By thine eyes the tempting booke
On which even crabbed old men looke
I sweare to thee, (though none abhorre them)
Yet I doe not love thee for them.

I doe not love thee for that faire,
Rich fanne of thy most curious haire;
Though the wires thereof be drawne
Finer then the threeds of lawne,
And are softer then the leaves
On which the subtle spinner weaues

I doe not love thee for those flowers,
Growing on thy cheeks (loves bowers)
Though such cunning them hath spread
None can paint them whit and red:
Loves golden arrowes thence are shot,
Yet for them I loue thee not

I doe not love thee for those soft,
Red corrall lips I've kist so oft;
Nor teeth of pearle, the double guard.
To speech, whence musicke still is heard:
Though from those lips a kisse being taken,
Might tyrants melt and death awaken.

I doe not love thee (o my fairest)
For that richest, for that rarest
Silver pilla0r which stands vnder
Thy sound head, that globe of wonder;
Though that neeke be whiter farre,
Then towers of pollisht Ivory are.

I doe not love thee for those mountaines
Hill'd with snow, whence milkey fountaines,
(Suger'd sweets, as sirropt berries)
Must one day run through pipes of cherries;
ô how much those breasts doe move me,
Yet for them I doe not love thee:

I doe not love thee for that belly,
Sleeke as satten, soft as jelly
Though within that Christall round
Heapes of treasure might be found,
So rich that for the best of them,
A King might leave his Diadem.

I doe not love thee for those thighes,
Whose Alablaster rocks doe use
So high and even that they stand
Like Sea-markes to some happy land.
Happy are those eyes have seene them,
More happy they that saile betweene them.

I love thee not for thy moist palme,
Though the dew thereof be balme:
Nor for thy pretty legge and foote,
Although it be the precious roote,
On which this goodly cedar growes,
(Sweete) I love thee not for those.

Nor for thy wit though pure and quicke,
Whose substance no arithmeticke
Can number downe: nor for those charmes
Mask't in thy embracing armes.
Though in them one night to lie,
Dearest I would gladly die

I love not for those eyes, nor haire,
Nor cheekes, nor lips, nor teeth so rare.
Nor for thy speech, thy necke, nor breast,
Nor for thy belly, nor the rest:
Nor for thy hand, nor foote so small,
But wouldst thou know (deere sweet) for all.

ANONYMOUS
17th Century

Love will find out the Way

OVER the mountains
      And over the waves,
Under the fountains
      And under the graves;
Under floods that are deepest,
      Which Neptune obey,
Over rocks that are steepest,
      Love will find out the way.

When there is no place
      For the glow-worm to lie,
When there is no space
      For receipt of a fly;
When the midge dares not venture
      Lest herself fast she lay,
If Love come, he will enter
      And will find out the way.

You may esteem him
      A child for his might;
Or you may deem him
      A coward for his flight;
But if she whom Love doth honour
      Be conceal'd from the day—
Set a thousand guards upon her,
      Love will find out the way.

Some think to lose him
      By having him confined;
And some do suppose him,
      Poor heart! to be blind;
But if ne'er so close ye wall him,
      Do the best that ye may,
Blind Love, if so ye call him,
      He will find out his way.

You may train the eagle
    To stoop to your fist;
Or you may inveigle
    The Phoenix of the east;
The lioness, you may move her
    To give over her prey;
But you'll ne'er stop a lover—
    He will find out the way.

If the earth it should part him,
    He would gallop it o'er;
If the seas should o'erthwart him,
    He would swim to the shore;
Should his Love become a swallow,
    Through the air to stray,
Love will lend wings to follow,
    And will find out the way.

There is no striving
    To cross his intent;
There is no contriving
    His plots to prevent;
But if once the message greet him
    That his True Love doth stay,
If Death should come and meet him,
    Love will find out the way!

ANNE BRADSTREET
(ca. 1612–1672)

To My Dear and Loving Husband

IF ever two were one, then surely we.
If ever man were lov'd by wife, then thee.
If ever wife was happy in a man,
Compare with me, ye women, if you can.
I prize thy love more than whole Mines of gold
Or all the riches that the East doth hold.
My love is such that Rivers cannot quench,
Nor ought but love from thee give recompetence.
Thy love is such I can no way repay.
The heavens reward thee manifold, I pray.
Then while we live, in love let's so persever
That when we live no more, we may live ever.

ANDREW MARVELL
(1621–1678)

The Definition of Love

MY Love is of a birth as rare
As 'tis for object strange and high.
It was begotten by despair
Upon Impossibility.

Magnanimous Despair alone
Could show me so divine a thing
Where feeble Hope could ne'er have flown,
But vainly flapp'd its Tinsel Wing.

And yet I quickly might arrive
Where my extended Soul is fixt,
But Fate does Iron wedges drive,
And always crowds itself betwixt.

For Fate with jealous Eye does see
Two perfect Loves; nor lets them close:
Their union would her ruin be,
And her Tyrannick pow'r depose.

And therefore her Decrees of Steel
Us as the distant poles have plac'd,
(Though Love's whole World on us doth wheel)
Not by themselves to be embrac'd.

Unless the giddy Heaven fall,
And earth some new Convulsion tear;
And, us to joyn, the World should all
Be cramp'd into a *Planisphere*.

As Lines, so Loves *oblique* may well
Themselves in every Angle greet;
But ours so truly *Paralel*,
Though infinite, can never meet.

Therefore the Love which us doth bind,
But Fate so enviously debars,
Is the Conjunction of the Mind,
And Opposition of the Stars.

The Fair Singer

TO make a final conquest of all me,
Love did compose so sweet an Enemy,
In whom both Beauties to my death agree,
Joyning themselves in fatal Harmony;
That while she with her Eyes my Heart does bind,
She with her Voice might captivate my Mind.

I could have fled from One but singly fair,
My dis-intangled soul it self might save,
Breaking the curled trammels of her hair.
But how should I avoid to be her Slave,
Whose subtle Art invisibly can wreath
My Fetters of the very Air I breath?

It had been easy fighting in some plain,
Where Victory might hang in equal choice,
But all resistance against her is vain,
Who has th'advantage both of Eyes and Voice,
And all my Forces needs must be undone,
She having gained both the Wind and Sun.

SIR CHARLES SEDLEY
(ca. 1639–1701)

Song from "The Mulberry Garden"

AH, *Chloris*, that I now could sit
　　As unconcern'd, as when
Your Infant Beauty could beget
　　No pleasure, nor no pain.

When I the dawn used to admire,
　　And prais'd the coming day;
I little thought the growing fire
　　Must take my Rest away.

Your Charms in harmless Childhood lay
　　Like metals in the mine,
Age from no face took more away,
　　Than Youth conceal'd in thine.

But as your Charms insensibly
　　To your perfection prest,
Fond Love as unperceiv'd did fly,
　　And in my Bosom rest.

My passion with your Beauty grew,
　　And *Cupid* at my heart,
Still as his mother favor'd you,
　　Threw a new flaming Dart.

Each glori'd in their wanton part,
　　To make a Lover he
Employ'd the utmost of his Art,
　　To make a Beauty she.

Though now I slowly bend to love,
　　Uncertain of my Fate,
If your fair self my Chains approve,
　　I shall my freedom hate.

Lovers, like dying men, may well
   At first disorder'd be,
Since none alive can truly tell
   What Fortune they must see.

Song

LOVE still has something of the Sea,
    From whence his Mother rose;
No time his Slaves from Doubt can free,
    Nor give their Thoughts repose;

They are becalm'd in clearest Days,
    And in rough Weather tost;
They wither under cold Delays,
    Or are in Tempests lost.

One while they seem to touch the Port,
    Then straight into the Main
Some angry Wind in cruel sport
    The Vessel drives again.

At first Disdain and Pride they fear,
    Which if they chance to 'scape,
Rivals and Falsehood soon appear
    In a more dreadful shape.

By such Degrees to Joy they come,
    And are so long withstood,
So slowly they recieve the Sum,
    It hardly does them good.

'Tis cruel to prolong a Pain,
    And to defer a Joy,
Believe, me, gentle *Celemene*,
    Offends the wingèd boy.

An hundred thousand Oaths your Fears
    Perhaps would not remove;
And if I gazed a thousand years
    I could no deeper love.

WILLIAM COWPER
(1731–1800)

Another.
Addressed To a Young Lady,

SWEET stream, that winds through yonder glade,
Apt emblem of a virtuous maid!
Silent and chaste she steals along,
Far from the world's gay busy throng,
With gentle yet prevailing force,
Intent upon her destined course;
Graceful and useful all she does,
Blessing and blest where'er she goes;
Pure-bosomed as that watery glass,
And Heaven reflected in her face!

To Mary

THE twentieth year is well-nigh past
Since first our sky was overcast;
Ah, would that this might be the last!
          My Mary!

Thy spirits have a fainter flow,
I see thee daily weaker grow;
'Twas my distress that brought thee low,
          My Mary!

Thy needles, once a shining store,
For my sake restless heretofore,
Now rust disused, and shine no more;
          My Mary!

For though thou gladly wouldst fulfil
The same kind office for me still,
Thy sight now seconds not thy will,
          My Mary!

But well thou playedst the housewife's part,
And all thy threads with magic art
Have wound themselves about this heart,
          My Mary!

Thy indistinct expressions seem
Like language uttered in a dream;
Yet me they charm, whate'er the theme,
          My Mary!

Thy silver locks, once auburn bright,
Are still more lovely in my sight
Than golden beams of orient light,
          My Mary!

For, could I view nor them nor thee,
What sight worth seeing could I see?
The sun would rise in vain for me,
                    My Mary!

Partakers of thy sad decline,
Thy hands their little force resign;
Yet, gently prest, press gently mine,
                    My Mary!

Such feebleness of limbs thou provest,
That now at every step thou movest
Upheld by two; yet still thou lovest,
                    My Mary!

And still to love, though prest with ill,
In wintry age to feel no chill,
With me is to be lovely still,
                    My Mary!

But ah! by constant heed I know,
How oft the sadness that I show
Transforms thy smiles to looks of woe,
                    My Mary!

And should my future lot be cast
With much resemblance of the past,
Thy worn-out heart will break at last,
                    My Mary!

SUSANNA BLAMIRE
(1747–1794)

The Recall To Affection

OH! stay Affection; pray thee stay!
What have I said—or meant to say?
'Twas love, e'en love the trespass caus'd
That warmth of speech, which scarce was clos'd
Ere the hard sentence tore my frame,
And dy'd my cheek with honest shame.
Regret came shivering through my veins,
And bound my tongue in iron chains;
My soul in prison seem'd to be,
And ever must if torn from thee;
One look of thine, when sweetly kind,
Can overturn a world of mind!
The stern resolves that pride has made,
At thy soft touch in vapour fade;
Thy smile, that rules the inmost soul,
Can every harsh resolve control.

Return, my lov'd companion dear,
The solace of each former year!
Else life, through many a sickening day,
Must slowly, slowly creep away;
E'en when thou bound'st this aching brow,
And sweetly cheer'd, I know not how,
Yet the dull hour, with weary knell,
Seem'd to toll on the passing bell.

If not for thee, this throbbing breast
Had ne'er enjoy'd the balm of rest;
Rest!—did I say? no bliss had known,
The blush of Nature by had flown,
Or o'er the senses vainly stray'd,
Hadst thou not wander'd in the shade;
Hadst thou not seen the clouds of morn,
On purple pinions lightly borne,
Uprear the canopy of day,

And o'er his chariot float away;
Hadst thou not mark'd the evening shade,
In all her changeful colours fade;—
The golden glow, the sapphire hue,
The rosy red, the melting blue,
The soft sea-green with yellow tinge,
The curling clouds with skirts of fringe;—
This eye had ne'er beheld one charm,
Or felt the glow of nature warm;
Nor had she seen one dropping shower
Bring back to life the fainting flower;
Or the tall woods their arches spread
In Gothic cloister over head;
While the pale moon, with lamp-like beam,
In tremors lent her silvery stream;
"Yon drops of flame that stud the sky"
Had seem'd plain stars to my poor eye,
Until these orbs, with glory bound,
By thee were call'd fair worlds around!

No; source of pleasure! 'twas thy soul
That brought me to conceive the whole.
The wish to please new thoughts inspir'd,
And I grew learn'd where thou admir'd;
To be companion meet I strove,
With all the self-taught lore of love,
Lov'd Nature as she ought to be;
For loving her, was loving thee!
But should'st thou leave this vacant heart,
And should we, should we ever part,
E'en Nature's self would grow less dear,
And I still shed the fretful tear.

MARY ROBINSON
(1758–1800)

Stanzas To Love

TELL me, Love, when I rove o'er some far distant plain,
    Shall I cherish the passion that dwells in my breast?
Or will Absence subdue the keen rigours of pain,
    And the swift wing of Time bring the balsam of
    rest?

Shall the image of him I was born to adore
    Inshrin'd in my bosom my idol still prove!
Or, seduced by caprice, shall fine feeling no more
    With the incense of truth gem the altar of Love?

When I view the deep tint of the dew-dropping rose,
    Where the bee sits enamour'd its nectar to sip;
Then, ah say! will not memory fondly disclose
    The softer vermilion that glow'd on his lip?

Will the Sun, when he rolls in his chariot of fire,
    So dazzle my mind with the glare of his rays,
That my senses one moment shall cease to admire
    The more perfect refulgence that beam'd in his
    lays?

When the shadows of twilight steal over the plain,
    And the Nightingale pours its lorn plaint in the
    grove;
Ah! will not the fondness that thrills thro' the strain,
    Then recall to my mind his dear accents of Love!

Then spare, thou sweet Urchin, thou soother of pain,
    Oh! spare the soft picture engrav'd on my heart;
As a record of Love let it ever remain;
    My bosom thy tablet—thy pencil a dart.

Stanzas: Written on the 14th of February, To My Once Dear Valentine

COME, Hope, and sweep the trembling string;
  Drop from thy pinions balm divine;
While, drooping o'er my lyre, I sing
  The graces of my Valentine.
Ah! Graces, fatal to my peace,
  Why round my heart your mischiefs twine?
Say, barb'rous Love, can aught increase
  The triumphs of my Valentine?

No more about my auburn hair
  The sparkling gems shall proudly vie;
The cypress, emblem of Despair,
  Shall there a faded chaplet die.
Young dimpled Pleasure quits my breast
  To seek some gaudier bow'r than mine,
Where low Caprice, by Fancy drest,
  Enthrals my truant Valentine.

The frozen brook, the mountain snow,
  The pearls that on the thistle shine,
The northern winds, that chilly blow,
  Are emblems of my Valentine.
Pale Sorrow sheds the quiv'ring flame
  That gleams on Truth's neglected shrine,
Fann'd by those sighs which still proclaim
  How much I love thee, Valentine!

Whene'er the icy hand of Death
  Shall grasp this sensate frame of mine,
On my cold lip the fleeting breath
  Shall murmur still—"dear Valentine!"
Then o'er my grave, ah! drop one tear,
  And sighing write this pensive line—
"A faithful heart lies mould'ring here,
  That well deserv'd its Valentine!"

To A Friend: (Who Asked The Author's Opinion of a Kiss)

"WHAT is a kiss?" 'tis but a seal
    That, warmly printed, soon decays;
'Tis but a zephyr taught to steal
    Where fleeting falsehood, smiling, plays.

The breeze will kiss the flow'r—but soon
    From flow'r to weed inconstant blows:
Such is the kiss of love, the boon
    Which fickle fancy oft bestows.

A perfum'd kiss once Venus gave
    The rose that caught her lover's sigh;
That rose with ev'ry gale wou'd wave,
    At ev'ry glance of morning die:

Would give its radiance to the beam
    Which glowing noon promiscuous threw;
Or to the twilight's parting gleam
    Would yield responsive tears of dew.

Oft to the bee its love would give,
    And breathe its odours wild around;
With honied sweets bid pleasure live,
    Or with its hidden mischiefs wound.

This rose was white, and to be blest,
    Around it insect myriads flew,
Charm'd by the wonders of its breast,
    Thrice essenc'd in the summer dew.

But when the lip of beauty shed
    A rival sweetness on that breast,
It blush'd, and droop'd its fragrant head,
    Asham'd to be so proudly blest.

Its colour chang'd, a crimson glow,
    Fix'd on its alter'd form, appears;
While round the sighing zephyrs blow,
    And nature bathes its leaves in tears.

Then, does not ev'ry kiss impart,
    In magic thrills of speechless pleasure,
Reproaches to the wand'ring heart,
    That knows not how to prize the treasure?

O yes! then let my bosom prove
    No throb—but friendship's throb divine;
And let the kiss of fickle love,
    Capricious monitor,—be thine!

Teach Me, Love, Since Thy Torments No Precepts Can Cure

TEACH me, love, since thy torments no precepts can cure,
    Since reflection and reason deny me relief;
Oh! teach me thy scorn and thy wrongs to endure,
    While the balm of resentment shall solace my grief.

Let my sighs never heave, let my tears never flow,
    Let the smile of contempt the stern victor defy;
For the tear has a charm which no art can bestow,
    And the language of love is the soul-breathing sigh.

Let me shun the proud despot who causes my care,
    Lest the torture I suffer should feed his disdain;
For my tyrant delights in the pang of despair,
    And the sound which he loves, is the deep groan of pain.

I will traverse the desert, climb mountains untrod,
    Where reflection shall sadden with legions of woes;
I will cool my scorch'd brain on the dew-moisten'd sod,
    While around my torn bosom the loud tempest blows.

Yet the mild breath of morning shall bid the storm fly,
    And the sun's glowing wreath shall encircle the steep;
But my bosom shall never forget the deep sigh,
    or my eyes lose their vision that prompts them to weep.

Then, oh! where shall I wander in search of repose?
    Where explore that oblivion that calms the wrung breast,—
Since the lover finds sorrow wherever he goes,
    And the world has for passion no pillow of rest?

Morning. Anacreontic.

THE sun now climbs the eastern hill;
    Awake, my love! thine eyes unclose!
Hark! near our hut the limpid rill
    Calls thee, soft tinkling, from repose!
The lark soars high above thy couch of rest;
    And on the plain the hunter's cries
Call echo from the misty skies:
Awake, my love! those glances meet,
Which promise hours of blisses sweet!

The dew-pearls fall from ev'ry flow'r—
    See how they glitter o'er the heath!
While balmy breathings fill the bow'r
    Where love still sighs with softer breath.
'Tis time to wake, my love! the day
    On sunny wing flies swift away:
Noon will thy velvet cheek annoy,
And ev'ning's dews will damp thy joy:
Then wake, my love! and ope thine eyes,
As bright, as blue, as summer skies!

We'll hunt the rein-deer, chase the boar,
    Thou shalt my Atalanta be!
And when our sportive toil is o'er,
    Venus shall snatch a grace from thee!
Young Bacchus shall his ivy band
    Receive from thy soft snowy hand;
And time his scythe aside shall fling,
While rosy rapture holds his wing:
Then wake, my love! the sun his beam
Darts golden on the rapid stream.

Thy cheek shall bloom, as Hebe's fair;
    Thy lip shall steep'd in honey be;
The graces shall entwine thy hair;
    The loves shall weave a zone for thee:
Thy feet shall bound across the waste,
    Like Daphne's by Apollo chas'd;
And ev'ry breeze that round thee blows,
Shall bring the fragrance of the rose.
Then come, my love! thy hours employ
No more in dreams—but wake to joy.

I hear thy voice, I see those orbs
    As blue, as brilliant as the day;
Thy vermil lip the dew absorbs,
    And scents thy breath like op'ning May:
Upon thy dimpled cheek the hue
    Of summer's blushing buds I view;
And on thy bosom's spotless glow,
The whiteness of the mountain snow:
Ah! close those eyes again—for see,
All nature is eclips'd by thee!

ROBERT BURNS
(1759–1796)

A Red, Red Rose

O, MY luve's like a red, red rose
That's newly sprung in June:
My luve's like the melodie
That's sweetly played in tune.

As fair art thou, my bonnie lass,
So deep in luve am I:
And I will luve thee still, my dear,
Till all the seas gang dry.

Till a' the seas gang dry, my dear,
And the rocks melt wi' the sun:
And I will luve thee still, my dear,
While the sands o' life shall run.

And fare thee weel, my only luve.
And fare thee weel awhile!
And I will come again, my luve,
Tho' it were ten thousand mile.

Forlorn My Love

FORLORN, my love, no comfort near,
Far, far from thee, I wander here;
Far, far from thee, the fate severe,
    At which I most repine, love.

CHORUS
O, wert thou, love, but near me,
But near, near, near me,
How kindly thou would cheer me,
    And mingle sighs with mine, love.

Around me scowls a wintry sky,
Blasting each bud of hope and joy;
And shelter, shade, nor home have I
    Save in these arms of thine, love.

CHORUS
O, wert thou, love, but near me,
But near, near, near me,
How kindly thou would cheer me,
    And mingle sighs with mine, love.

Cold, alter'd friendship's cruel part,
To poison Fortune's ruthless dart –
Let me not break thy faithful heart,
    And say that fate is mine, love.

CHORUS
O, wert thou, love, but near me,
But near, near, near me,
How kindly thou would cheer me,
    And mingle sighs with mine, love.

But, dreary tho' the moments fleet,
O, let me think we yet shall meet!
That only ray of solace sweet
    Can on thy Chloris shine, love.

CHORUS

O, wert thou, love, but near me,
But near, near, near me,
How kindly thou would cheer me,
    And mingle sighs with mine, love.

Ae Fond Kiss

AE fond kiss, and then we sever!
Ae fareweel, alas, for ever!
Deepin heart-wrung tears I'll pledge thee,
Warring sighs and groans I'll wage thee.
Who shall say that Fortune grieves him,
While the star of hope she leaves him?
Me, nae cheerfu' twinkle lights me,
Dark despair around benights me.

I'll ne'er blame my partial fancy,
Naething could resist my Nancy;
But to see her was to love her;
Love but her, and love forever.
Had we never lov'd sae kindly,
Had we never lov'd sae blindly,
Never met – or never parted,
We had ne'er been broken-hearted.

Fare thee weel, thou first and fairest!
Fare thee weel, thou best and dearest!
Thine be ilka joy and treasure,
Peace, enjoyment, love, and pleasure!
Ae fond kiss, and then we sever;
Ae fareweel, alas, for ever!
Deep in heart-wrung tears I'll pledge thee,
Warring sighs and groans I'll wage thee!

SAMUEL ROGERS
(1763–1855)

On . . Asleep.

SLEEP on, and dream of Heaven awhile.
Tho' shut so close thy laughing eyes,
Thy rosy lips still wear a smile,
And move, and breathe delicious sighs! –

Ah, now soft blushes tinge her cheeks
And mantle o'er her neck of snow.
Ah, now she murmurs, now she speaks
What most I wish—and fear to know.

She starts, she trembles, and she weeps!
Her fair hands folded on her breast.
—And now, how like a saint she sleeps!
A seraph in the realms of rest!

Sleep on secure! Above control,
Thy thoughts belong to Heaven and thee!
And may the secret of thy soul
Remain within its sanctuary!

WILLIAM WORDSWORTH
(1770–1850)

She Was a Phantom of Delight

SHE was a Phantom of delight
When first she gleam'd upon my sight;
A lovely Apparition, sent
To be a moment's ornament:
Her eyes as stars of twilight fair;
Like twilight's, too, her dusky hair;
But all things else about her drawn
From May-time and the cheerful Dawn;
A dancing Shape, an Image gay,
To haunt, to startle, and way-lay.

I saw her upon nearer view,
A Spirit, yet a Woman too!
Her household motions light and free,
And steps of virgin liberty;
A countenance in which did meet
Sweet records, promises as sweet;
A Creature not too bright or good
For human nature's daily food,
For transient sorrows, simple wiles,
Praise, blame, love, kisses, tears, and smiles.

And now I see with eye serene
The very pulse of the machine;
A Being breathing thoughtful breath,
A Traveller betwixt life and death:
The reason firm, the temperate will,
Endurance, foresight, strength, and skill;
A perfect Woman, nobly plann'd
To warn, to comfort, and command;
And yet a Spirit still, and bright
With something of an angel light.

To —— *[Let other bards of angels sing]*

LET other bards of angels sing,
    Bright suns without a spot;
But thou art no such perfect thing:
    Rejoice that thou art not!

Heed not tho' none should call thee fair;
    So, Mary, let it be
If nought in loveliness compare
    With what thou art to me.

True beauty dwells in deep retreats,
    Whose veil is unremoved
Till heart with heart in concord beats,
    And the lover is beloved.

SAMUEL TAYLOR COLERIDGE
(1772-1834)

Love

ALL thoughts, all passions, all delights,
Whatever stirs this mortal frame,
All are but ministers of Love,
    And feed his sacred flame.

Oft in my waking dreams do I
Live o'er again that happy hour,
When midway on the mount I lay,
    Beside the ruined tower.

The moonshine, stealing o'er the scene
Had blended with the lights of eve;
And she was there, my hope, my joy,
    My own dear Genevieve!

She leant against the armed man,
The statue of the armed knight;
She stood and listened to my lay,
    Amid the lingering light.

Few sorrows hath she of her own,
My hope! my joy! my Genevieve!
She loves me best, whene'er I sing
    The songs that make her grieve.

I played a soft and doleful air,
I sang an old and moving story—
An old rude song, that suited well
    That ruin wild and hoary.

She listened with a flitting blush,
With downcast eyes and modest grace;
For well she knew, I could not choose
    But gaze upon her face.

I told her of the Knight that wore
Upon his shield a burning brand;
And that for ten long years he wooed
    The Lady of the Land.

I told her how he pined: and ah!
The deep, the low, the pleading tone
With which I sang another's love,
    Interpreted my own.

She listened with a flitting blush,
With downcast eyes, and modest grace;
And she forgave me, that I gazed
    Too fondly on her face!

But when I told the cruel scorn
That crazed that bold and lovely Knight,
And that he crossed the mountain-woods,
    Nor rested day nor night;

That sometimes from the savage den,
And sometimes from the darksome shade,
And sometimes starting up at once
    In green and sunny glade,–

There came and looked him in the face
An angel beautiful and bright;
And that he knew it was a Fiend,
    This miserable Knight!

And that unknowing what he did,
He leaped amid a murderous band,
And saved from outrage worse than death
    The Lady of the Land!

And how she wept, and clasped his knees;
And how she tended him in vain–
And ever strove to expiate
    The scorn that crazed his brain;–

And that she nursed him in a cave;
And how his madness went away,
When on the yellow forest-leaves
    A dying man he lay;–

His dying words–but when I reached
That tenderest strain of all the ditty,
My faltering voice and pausing harp
    Disturbed her soul with pity!

All impulses of soul and sense
Had thrilled my guileless Genevieve;
The music and the doleful tale,
    The rich and balmy eve;

And hopes, and fears that kindle hope,
An undistinguishable throng,
And gentle wishes long subdued,
    Subdued and cherished long!

She wept with pity and delight,
She blushed with love, and virgin-shame;
And like the murmur of a dream,
    I heard her breathe my name.

Her bosom heaved–she stepped aside,
As conscious of my look she stepped–
Then suddenly, with timorous eye
    She fled to me and wept.

She half enclosed me with her arms,
She pressed me with a meek embrace;
And bending back her head, looked up,
    And gazed upon my face.

'Twas partly love, and partly fear,
And partly 'twas a bashful art,
That I might rather feel, than see,
    The swelling of her heart.

I calmed her fears, and she was calm,
And told her love with virgin pride;
And so I won my Genevieve,
    My bright and beauteous Bride.

The Exchange

WE pledged our hearts, my love and I –
    I in my arms the maiden clasping;
I could not guess the reason why,
    But, oh! I trembled like an aspen.

Her father's love she bade me gain;
    I went, but shook like any reed!
I strove to act the man–in vain!
    We had exchanged our hearts indeed.

An Angel Visitant

WITHIN these circling hollies woodbine–clad–
Beneath this small blue roof of vernal sky–
How warm, how still! Tho' tears should dim mine eye,
Yet will my heart for days continue glad,
For here, my love, thou art, and here am I!

THOMAS MOORE
(1779–1852)

The Kiss

GROW to my lip, thou sacred kiss,
On which my soul's beloved swore
That there should come a time of bliss,
When she would mock my hopes no more.
And fancy shall thy glow renew,
In sighs at morn, and dreams at night,
And none shall steal thy holy dew
Till thou'rt absolv'd by rapture's rite.
Sweet hours that are to make me blest,
Fly, swift as breezes, to the goal,
And let my love, my more than soul
Come blushing to this ardent breast.
Then, while in every glance I drink
The rich o'erflowings of her mind,
Oh! let her all enamour'd sink
In sweet abandonment resign'd,
Blushing for all our struggles past,
And murmuring, "I am thine at last!"

If I Were Yonder Wave, My Dear

IF I were yonder wave, my dear,
    And thou the isle it clasps around,
I would not let a foot come near
    My land of bliss, my fairy ground.

If I were yonder conch of gold,
    And thou the pearl within it plac'd.
I would not let an eye behold
    The sacred gem my arms embrac'd.

If I were yonder orange-tree,
    And thou the blossom blooming there,
I would not yield a breath of thee
    To scent the most imploring air.

Oh! bend not o'er the water's brink,
    Give not the wave that odorous sigh,
Nor let its burning mirror drink
    The soft reflection of thine eye.

That glossy hair, that glowing cheek,
    So pictur'd in the waters seem,
That I could gladly plunge to seek
    Thy image in the glassy stream.

Blest fate! at once my chilly grave
    And nuptial bed that stream might be;
I'll wed thee in its mimic wave,
    And die upon the shade of thee.

Behold the leafy mangrove, bending
    O'er the waters blue and bright,
Like Nea's silky lashes, lending
    Shadow to her eyes of light.

Oh, my belov'd! where'er I turn,
    Some trace of thee enchants mine eyes;
In every star thy glances burn;
    Thy blush on every flow'ret lies.

Nor find I in creation aught
    Of bright, or beautiful, or rare,
Sweet to the sense, or pure to thought,
    But thou art found reflected there.

Oh, No – Not Ev'n When We First Loved

OH, NO –not ev'n when first we lov'd,
    Wert thou as dear as now thou art;
Thy beauty then my senses mov'd,
    But now thy virtues bind my heart.
What was but Passion's sigh before,
    Has since been turn'd to Reason's vow;
And, though I then might love thee *more*,
    Trust me, I love thee *better* now.

Although my heart in earlier youth
    Might kindle with more wild desire,
Believe me, it has gain'd in truth
    Much more than it has lost in fire.
The flame now warms my inmost core,
    That then but sparkled o'er my brow,
And, though I seem'd to love thee more,
    Yet, oh, I love thee better now.

GEORGE GORDON, LORD BYRON
(1788–1824)

She Walks in Beauty

SHE walks in beauty, like the night
   Of cloudless climes and starry skies;
And all that's best of dark and bright
   Meet in her aspect and her eyes:
Thus mellow'd to that tender light
   Which heaven to gaudy day denies.

One shade the more, one ray the less,
   Had half impair'd the nameless grace
Which waves in every raven tress,
   Or softly lightens o'er her face;
Where thoughts serenely sweet express
   How pure, how dear their dwelling-place.

And on that cheek, and o'er that brow,
   So soft, so calm, yet eloquent,
The smiles that win, the tints that glow,
   But tell of days in goodness spent,
A mind at peace with all below,
   A heart whose love is innocent!

Stanzas Written on the Road between Florence and Pisa

OH TALK not to me of a name great in story;
The days of our youth are the days of our glory;
And the myrtle and ivy of sweet two-and-twenty
Are worth all your laurels, though ever so plenty.

What are garlands and crowns to the brow that is wrinkled?
'Tis but as a dead flower with May-dew besprinkled:
Then away with all such from the head that is hoary!
What care I for the wreaths that can only give glory?

Oh Fame! – if I e'er took delight in thy praises,
'Twas less for the sake of thy high-sounding phrases,
Than to see the bright eyes of the dear one discover
She thought that I was not unworthy to love her.

There chiefly I sought thee, *there* only I found thee;
Her glance was the best of the rays that surround thee;
When it sparkled o'er aught that was bright in my story,
I knew it was love, and I felt it was glory.

To Woman

WOMAN! experience might have told me
That all must love thee who behold thee:
Surely experience might have taught
Thy firmest promises are nought;
But, placed in all thy charms before me,
All I forget, but to adore thee.
Oh memory! thou choicest blessing,
When joined with hope, when still possessing;
But how much cursed by every lover
When hope is fled, and passion's over.
Woman, that fair and fond deceiver,
How prompt are striplings to believe her!
How throbs the pulse, when first we view
The eye that rolls in glossy blue,
Or sparkles black, or mildly throws
A beam from under hazel brows!
How quick we credit every oath,
And hear her plight the willing troth!
Fondly we hope 't will last for aye,
When, lo! she changes in a day.
This record will for ever stand,
"Woman, thy vows are traced in sand."

To A Lady

OH! had my fate been join'd with thine,
    As once this pledge appear'd a token,
These follies had not then been mine,
    For then my peace had not been broken.

To thee these early faults I owe,
    To thee, the wise and old reproving:
They know my sins, but do not know
    'Twas thine to break the bonds of loving.

For once my soul, like thine, was pure,
    And all its rising fires could smother;
But now thy vows no more endure,
    Bestow'd by thee upon another.

Perhaps his peace I could destroy,
    And spoil the blisses that await him;
Yet let my rival smile in joy,
    For thy dear sake I cannot hate him.

Ah! since thy angel form is gone,
    My heart no more can rest with any;
But what it sought in thee alone,
    Attempts, alas! to find in many.

Then, fare thee well, deceitful Maid!
    'Twere vain and fruitless to regret thee;
Nor Hope, nor Memory yield their aid,
    But Pride may teach me to forget thee.

Yet all this giddy waste of years,
    This tiresome round of palling pleasures;
These varied loves, these matrons' fears,
    These thoughtless strains to Passion's measures—

If thou wert mine, had all been hush'd:–
    This cheek, now pale from early riot,
With Passion's hectic ne'er had flush'd,
    But bloom'd in calm domestic quiet.

Yes, once the rural scene was sweet,
    For Nature seem'd to smile before thee;
And once my Breast abhorr'd deceit,–
    For then it beat but to adore thee.

But, now, I seek for other joys:
    To think, would drive my soul to madness;
In thoughtless throngs, and empty noise,
    I conquer half my Bosom's sadness.

Yet, even in these, a thought will steal,
    In spite of every vain endeavour;
And fiends might pity what I feel, –
    To know that thou art lost for ever.

When We Two Parted

WHEN we two parted
   In silence and tears,
Half broken-hearted
   To sever for years,
Pale grew thy cheek and cold,
   Colder thy kiss;
Truly that hour foretold
   Sorrow to this.

The dew of the morning
   Sunk chill on my brow—
It felt like the warning
   Of what I feel now.
Thy vows are all broken,
   And light is thy fame:
I hear thy name spoken,
   And share in its shame.

They name thee before me,
   A knell to mine ear;
A shudder comes o'er me—
   Why wert thou so dear?
They know not I knew thee,
   Who knew thee too well:
Long, long shall I rue thee,
   Too deeply to tell.

In secret we met—
   In silence I grieve,
That thy heart could forget,
   Thy spirit deceive.
If I should meet thee
   After long years,
How should I greet thee?
   With silence and tears.

Stanzas for Music

THERE be none of Beauty's daughters
    With a magic like thee;
And like music on the waters
    Is thy sweet voice to me:
When, as if its sound were causing
The charmèd ocean's pausing,
The waves lie still and gleaming,
And the lull'd winds seem dreaming:

And the midnight moon is weaving
    Her bright chain o'er the deep,
Whose breast is gently heaving
    As an infant's asleep:
So the sprit bows before thee,
To listen and adore thee;
With a full but soft emotion,
Like the swell of Summer's ocean.

PERCY BYSSHE SHELLEY
(1792-1822)

Love's Philosophy

THE fountains mingle with the river
　　And the rivers with the ocean,
The winds of heaven mix for ever
　　With a sweet emotion;
Nothing in the world is single;
　　All things by a law divine
In one another's being mingle—
　　Why not I with thine?

See the mountains kiss high heaven,
　　And the waves clasp one another;
No sister flower would be forgiven
　　If it disdain'd its brother;
And the sunlight clasps the earth,
　　And the moonbeams kiss the sea:
What are all these kissings worth,
　　If thou kiss not me?

To Jane

THE keen stars were twinkling,
And the fair moon was rising among them,
Dear Jane.
The guitar was tinkling,
But the notes were not sweet till you sung them
Again.

As the moon's soft splendour
O'er the faint cold starlight of Heaven
Is thrown,
So your voice most tender
To the strings without soul had then given
Its own.

The stars will awaken,
Though the moon sleep a full hour later
To-night;
No leaf will be shaken
Whilst the dews of your melody scatter
Delight.

Though the sound overpowers,
Sing again, with your dear voice revealing
A tone
Of some world far from ours,
Where music and moonlight and feeling
Are one.

The Indian Serenade

I ARISE from dreams of thee
In the first sweet sleep of night,
When the winds are breathing low,
And the stars are shining bright;
I arise from dreams of thee,
And a spirit in my feet
Hath led me—who knows how?
To thy chamber window, sweet!

The wandering airs they faint
On the dark, the silent stream-
The champak odors fail
Like sweet thoughts in a dream;
The Nightingale's complaint,
It dies upon her heart,
As I must on thine,
Oh, belovèd as thou art!

Oh lift me from the grass!
I die! I faint! I fail!
Let thy love in kisses rain
On my lips and eyelids pale.
My cheek is cold and white, alas!
My heart beats loud and fast,
Oh! press it to thine own again,
Where it will break at last.

To Harriet

THY look of love has power to calm
    The stormiest passion of my soul;
Thy gentle words are drops of balm
    In life's too bitter bowl;
No grief is mine, but that alone
These choicest blessings I have known.

Harriet! if all who long to live
    In the warm sunshine of thine eye,
That price beyond all pain must give,–
    Beneath thy scorn to die;
Then hear thy chosen own too late
His heart most worthy of thy hate.

Be thou, then, one among mankind
    Whose heart is harder not for state,
Thou only virtuous, gentle, kind,
    Amid a world of hate;
And by a slight endurance seal
A fellow-being's lasting weal.

For pale with anguish is his cheek,
    His breath comes fast, his eyes are dim,
Thy name is struggling ere he speak,
    Weak is each trembling limb;
In mercy let him not endure
The misery of a fatal cure.

Oh, trust for once no erring guide!
    Bid the remorseless feeling flee;
'Tis malice, 'tis revenge, 'tis pride,
    'Tis anything but thee;
Oh, deign a nobler pride to prove,
And pity if thou canst not love.

To —

WHEN passion's trance is overpast,
If tenderness and truth could last,
Or live, whilst all wild feelings keep
Some mortal slumber, dark and deep,
I should not weep, I should not weep!

It were enough to feel, to see,
Thy soft eyes gazing tenderly,
And dream the rest – and burn and be
The secret food of fires unseen,
Couldst thou but be as thou hast been.

After the slumber of the year
The woodland violets reappear;
All things revive in field or grove,
And sky and sea, but two, which move
And form all others, life and love.

To The Queen of My Heart

SHALL we roam, my love,
To the twilight grove,
When the moon is rising bright;
Oh, I'll whisper there,
In the cool night-air,
What I dare not in broad daylight!

I'll tell thee a part
Of the thoughts that start
To being when thou art nigh;
And thy beauty, more bright
Than the stars' soft light,
Shall seem as a weft from the sky.

When the pale moonbeam
On tower and stream
Sheds a flood of silver sheen,
How I love to gaze
As the cold ray strays
O'er thy face, my heart's throned queen!

Wilt thou roam with me
To the restless sea,
And linger upon the steep,
And list to the flow
Of the waves below
How they toss and roar and leap?

Those boiling waves,
And the storm that raves
At night o'er their foaming crest,
Resemble the strife
That, from earliest life,
The passions have waged in my breast.

Oh, come then, and rove
To the sea or the grove,
When the moon is rising bright;
And I'll whisper there,
In the cool night-air,
What I dare not in broad daylight.

WILLIAM CULLEN BRYANT
(1794–1878)

Song

DOST thou idly ask to hear
    At what gentle seasons
Nymphs relent, when lovers near
    Press the tenderest reasons?
Ah, they give their faith too oft
    To the careless wooer;
Maidens' hearts are always soft:
    Would that men's were truer!

Woo the fair one when around
    Early birds are singing;
When, o'er all the fragrant ground,
    Early herbs are springing:
When the brookside, bank, and grove,
    All with blossoms laden,
Shine with beauty, breathe of love,–
    Woo the timid maiden.

Woo her when, with rosy blush,
    Summer eve is sinking;
When, on rills that softly gush,
    Stars are softly winking;
When through boughs that knit the bower
    Moonlight gleams are stealing;
Woo her, till the gentle hour
    Wake a gentler feeling.

Woo her when autumnal dyes
    Tinge the woody mountain;
When the dropping foliage lies
    In the weedy fountain;
Let the scene, that tells how fast
    Youth is passing over,
Warn her, ere her bloom is past,
    To secure her lover.

Woo her when the north winds call
    At the lattice nightly;
When, within the cheerful hall,
    Blaze the fagots brightly;
While the wintry tempest round
    Sweeps the landscape hoary,
Sweeter in her ear shall sound
    Love's delightful story.

The Arctic Lover

GONE is the long, long winter night,
  Look, my belovèd one!
How glorious, through his depths of light,
  Rolls the majestic sun!
The willows, waked from winter's death,
Give out a fragrance like thy breath—
  The summer is begun!

Ay, 'tis the long bright summer day:
  Hark to that mighty crash!
The loosened ice-ridge breaks away—
  The smitten waters flash.
Seaward the glittering mountain rides,
While, down its green translucent sides,
  The foamy torrents dash.

See, love, my boat is moored for thee
  By ocean's weedy floor—
The petrel does not skim the sea
  More swiftly than my oar.
We'll go where, on the rocky isles,
Her eggs the screaming sea-fowl piles
  Beside the pebbly shore.

Or, bide thou where the poppy blows,
  With wind-flowers frail and fair,
While I, upon his isle of snow,
  Seek and defy the bear.
Fierce though he be, and huge of frame,
This arm his savage strength shall tame,
  And drag him from his lair.

When crimson sky and flamy cloud
    Bespeak the summer o'er,
And the dead valleys wear a shroud
    Of snows that melt no more,
I'll build of ice thy winter home,
With glistening walls and glassy dome,
    And spread with skins the floor.

The white fox by thy couch shall play;
    And, from the frozen skies,
The meteors of a mimic day
    Shall flash upon thine eyes.
And I—for such thy vow—meanwhile
Shall hear thy voice and see thy smile,
    Till that long midnight flies.

JOHN KEATS
(1795–1821)

Ode to Psyche

O GODDESS! hear these tuneless numbers, wrung
    By sweet enforcement and remembrance dear,
And pardon that thy secrets should be sung
    Even into thine own soft-conched ear:
Surely I dream'd to-day, or did I see
    The winged Psyche with awaken'd eyes?
I wander'd in a forest thoughtlessly,
    And, on the sudden, fainting with surprise,
Saw two fair creatures, couched side by side
    In deepest grass, beneath the whisp'ring roof
    Of leaves and trembled blossoms, where there ran
    A brooklet, scarce espied:

'Mid hush'd, cool-rooted flowers, fragrant-eyed,
    Blue, silver-white, and budded Tyrian
They lay calm-breathing on the bedded grass;
    Their arms embraced, and their pinions too;
    Their lips touch'd not, but had not bade adieu,
As if disjoined by soft-handed slumber,
And ready still past kisses to outnumber
    At tender eye-dawn of aurorean love:
    The winged boy I knew;
    But who wast thou, O happy, happy dove?
    His Psyche true!

O latest-born and loveliest vision far
    Of all Olympus' faded hierarchy!
Fairer than Phoebe's sapphire-region'd star,
    Or Vesper, amorous glow-worm of the sky;
Fairer than these, though temple thou hast none,
    Nor altar heap'd with flowers;
Nor virgin-choir to make delicious moan
    Upon the midnight hours;
No voice, no lute, no pipe, no incense sweet
    From chain-swung censer teeming;

No shrine, no grove, no oracle, no heat
    Of pale-mouth'd prophet dreaming.

O brightest! though too late for antique vows,
    Too, too late for the fond believing lyre,
When holy were the haunted forest boughs,
    Holy the air, the water, and the fire;
Yet even in these days so far retired
    From happy pieties, thy lucent fans,
    Fluttering among the faint Olympians,
I see, and sing, by my own eyes inspired.
So let me be thy choir, and make a moan
    Upon the midnight hours;
Thy voice, thy lute, thy pipe, thy incense sweet
    From swinged censer teeming:
Thy shrine, thy grove, thy oracle, thy heat
    Of pale-mouth'd prophet dreaming.

Yes, I will be thy priest, and build a fane
    In some untrodden region of my mind,
Where branched thoughts, new grown with pleasant
    pain,
    Instead of pines shall murmur in the wind:
Far, far around shall those dark-cluster'd trees
    Fledge the wild-ridged mountains steep by steep;
And there by zephyrs, streams, and birds, and bees,
    The moss-lain Dryads shall be lull'd to sleep;
And in the midst of this wide quietness
A rosy sanctuary will I dress
With the wreath'd trellis of a working brain,
    With buds, and bells, and stars without a name,
With all the gardener Fancy e'er could feign,
    Who breeding flowers, will never breed the same:
And there shall be for thee all soft delight
    That shadowy thought can win,
A bright torch, and a casement ope at night,
    To let the warm Love in!

Asleep! O sleep a little while, white pearl!

ASLEEP! O sleep a little while, white pearl!
And let me kneel, and let me pray to thee,
And let me call Heaven's blessing on thine eyes,
And let me breathe into the happy air,
That doth enfold and touch thee all about,
Vows of my slavery, my giving up,
My sudden adoration, my great love!

When I Have Fears
That I May Cease To Be

WHEN I have fears that I may cease to be
    Before my pen has glean'd my teeming brain,
Before high piled books, in charact'ry,
    Hold like rich garners the full-ripen'd grain;
When I behold, upon the night's starr'd face,
    Huge cloudy symbols of a high romance,
And think that I may never live to trace
    Their shadows, with the magic hand of chance;
And when I feel, fair creature of an hour!
    That I shall never look upon thee more,
Never have relish in the faery power
    Of unreflecting love; — then on the shore
Of the wide world I stand alone, and think
    Till Love and Fame to nothingness do sink.

Woman! When I Behold Thee Flippant, Vain

WOMAN! when I behold thee flippant, vain,
    Inconstant, childish, proud, and full of fancies;
    Without that modest softening that enhances
The downcast eye, repentant of the pain
That its mild light creates to heal again:
    E'en then, elate, my spirit leaps, and prances,
    E'en then my soul with exultation dances
For that to love, so long, I've dormant lain:
But when I see thee meek, and kind, and tender,
    Heavens! how desperately do I adore
Thy winning graces;—to be thy defender
    I hotly burn—to be a Calidore—
A very Red Cross Knight—a stout Leander—
    Might I be loved by thee like these of yore.

Light feet, dark violet eyes, and parted hair;
    Soft dimpled hands, white neck, and creamy breast,
    Are things on which the dazzled senses rest
Till the fond, fixed eyes, forget they stare.
From such fine pictures, heavens! I cannot dare
    To turn my admiration, though unpossess'd
    They be of what is worthy,—though not drest
In lovely modesty, and virtues rare.
Yet these I leave as thoughtless as a lark;
    These lures I straight forget—e'en ere I dine,
Or thrice my palate moisten: but when I mark
    Such charms with mild intelligences shine,
My ear is open like a greedy shark,
    To catch the tunings of a voice divine.

Ah! who can e'er forget so fair a being?
    Who can forget her half retiring sweets?
    God! she is like a milk-white lamb that bleats
For man's protection. Surely the All-seeing,
Who joys to see us with his gifts agreeing,
    Will never give him pinions, who intreats
    Such innocence to ruin,—who vilely cheats

A dove-like bosom. In truth there is no freeing
One's thoughts from such a beauty; when I hear
    A lay that once I saw her hand awake,
Her form seems floating palpable, and near;
    Had I e'er seen her from an arbour take
A dewy flower, oft would that hand appear,
    And o'er my eyes the trembling moisture shake.

Unfelt, Unheard, Unseen

UNFELT, unheard, unseen,
I've left my little queen,
Her languid arms in silver slumber lying:
    Ah! through their nestling touch,
    Who—who could tell how much
There is for madness—cruel, or complying?

    Those faery lids how sleek!
    Those lips how moist!—they speak,
In ripest quiet, shadows of sweet sounds:
    Into my fancy's ear
    Melting a burden dear,
How 'Love doth know no fullness nor no bounds.'

    True!—tender monitors!
    I bend unto your laws:
This sweetest day for dalliance was born!
    So, without more ado,
    I'll feel my heaven anew,
For all the blushing of the hasty morn.

Modern Love

AND what is love? It is a doll dress'd up
For idleness to cosset, nurse, and dandle;
A thing of soft misnomers, so divine
That silly youth doth think to make itself
Divine by loving, and so goes on
Yawning and doting a whole summer long,
Till Miss's comb is made a pearl tiara,
And common Wellingtons turn Romeo boots;
Then Cleopatra lives at number seven,
And Antony resides in Brunswick Square.
Fools! if some passions high have warm'd the world,
If Queens and Soldiers have play'd deep for hearts,
It is no reason why such agonies
Should be more common than the growth of weeds.
Fools! make me whole again that weighty pearl
The Queen of Egypt melted, and I'll say
That ye may love in spite of beaver hats.

Ode To Fanny

PHYSICIAN Nature! let my spirit blood!
   O ease my heart of verse and let me rest;
Throw me upon thy Tripod, till the flood
     Of stifling numbers ebbs from my full breast.
        A theme! a theme! great nature! give a theme;
       Let me begin my dream.
I come—I see thee, as thou standest there,
Beckon me not into the wintry air.

Ah! dearest love, sweet home of all my fears,
    And hopes, and joys, and panting miseries,—
To-night, if I may guess, thy beauty wears
       A smile of such delight,
       As brilliant and as bright,
     As when with ravished, aching, vassal eyes,
       Lost in soft amaze,
       I gaze, I gaze!
0
Who now, with greedy looks, eats up my feast?
    What stare outfaces now my silver moon!
Ah! keep that hand unravished at the least;
       Let, let, the amorous burn—
       But, pr'ythee, do not turn
     The current of your heart from me so soon.
       O! save, in charity,
       The quickest pulse for me.

Save it for me, sweet love! though music breathe
    Voluptuous visions into the warm air;
Though swimming through the dance's dangerous
    wreath,
       Be like an April day,
       Smiling and cold and gay,
     A temperate lily, temperate as fair;
       Then, Heaven! there will be
       A warmer June for me.

Why, this—you'll say, my Fanny! is not true:
　　Put your soft hand upon your snowy side,
Where the heart beats: confess—'tis nothing new—
　　　　Must not a woman be
　　　　A feather on the sea,
　　Sway'd to and fro by every wind and tide?
　　　　Of as uncertain speed
　　　　As blow-ball from the mead?

I know it—and to know it is despair
　　To one who loves you as I love, sweet Fanny:
Whose heart goes fluttering for you every where,
　　　　Nor, when away you roam,
　　　　Dare keep its wretched home:
　　Love, love alone, his pains severe and many:
　　　　Then, loveliest! keep me free,
　　　　From torturing jealousy.

Ah! if you prize my subdued soul above
　　The poor, the fading, brief, pride of an hour;
Let none profane my Holy See of love,
　　　　Or with a rude hand break
　　　　The sacramental cake:
　　Let none else touch the just new-budded flower;
　　　　If not—may my eyes close,
　　　　Love! on their lost repose.

JAMES GATES PERCIVAL
(1795-1856)

The Serenade

SOFTLY the moonlight
Is shed on the lake,
Cool is the summer night,–
Wake! O awake!
Faintly the curfew
Is heard from afar,
List ye! O list!
To the lively guitar.

Trees cast a mellow shade
Over the vale,
Sweetly the serenade
Breathes in the gale,
Softly and tenderly
Over the lake,
Gayly and cheerily,–
Wake! O awake!

See the light pinnace
Draws nigh to the shore,
Swiftly it glides
At the heave of the oar,
Cheerily plays
On its buoyant car,
Nearer and nearer,
The lively guitar.

Now the wind rises
And ruffles the pine,
Ripples foam-crested
Like diamonds shine,
They flash, where the waters
The white pebbles lave,
In the wake of the moon,
As it crosses the wave.

Bounding from billow
To billow, the boat
Like a wild swan is seen
On the waters to float;
And the light dripping oars
Bear it smoothly along
In time to the air
Of the gondolier's song.

And high on the stern
Stands the young and the brave,
As love-led he crosses
The star-spangled wave,
And blends with the murmur
Of water and grove
The tones of the night,
That are sacred to love.

His gold-hilted sword
At his bright belt is hung,
His mantle of silk
On his shoulder is flung,
And high waves the feather,
That dances and plays
On his cap where the buckle
And rosary blaze.

The maid from her lattice
Looks down on the lake,
To see the foam sparkle,
The bright billow break,
And to hear in his boat,
Where he shines like a star,
Her lover so tenderly
Touch his guitar.

She opens her lattice,
And sits in the glow
Of the moonlight and starlight,
A statue of snow;
And she sings in a voice
That is broken with sighs,
And she darts on her lover
The light of her eyes.

His love-speaking pantomime
Tells her his soul,—
How wild in that sunny clime
Hearts and eyes roll.
She waves with her white hand
Her white fazzolet,
And her burning thoughts flash
From her eyes' living jet.

The moonlight is hid
In a vapor of snow;
Her voice and his rebeck
Alternately flow;
Re-echoed they swell
From the rock on the hill;
They sing their farewell,
And the music is still.

The Lover's Lament

O, closed the eye that beamed so kindly,
Mild as the morn, when it first uncloses!
O, pale the lip, that smiled so fondly,
Pure, in its hue, as the dewy rose!
O, like the rose, that lip has faded!
Cold in the grave thy form reposes;
Dark, dark as night, my soul is shaded;
Full as the fountain, my heart now flows.

Long shall I think of the hours when I sat with thee.
Under the shade of the trysting tree, at silent gloaming;
Long shall I dwell on the scenes I have viewed with thee;
But I shall see thee no more again.
Yet shall I never forget how I strayed with thee,
Over the hills, in the sunny noon of April, roaming;
Never forget how in childhood I played with thee,
Hours, that, like thee, were without a stain.

GEORGE POPE MORRIS
(1802-1864)

Venetian Serenade

COME, come to me, love!
　　Come, love!-Arise!
And shame the bright stars
　　With the light of thine eyes;
Look out from thy lattice-
　　Oh, lady-bird, hear!
A swan on the water-
　　My gondola's near!

Come, come to me, love!
　　Come, love!-My bride!
O'er crystal in moonbeams
　　We'll tranquilly glide,
In the dip of the oar
　　A melody flows
Sweet as the nightingale
　　Sings to the rose.

Come, come to me, love!
　　Come, love!-The day
Brings warder and cloister!
　　Away, then-away!
Oh, haste to thy lover!
　　Not yon star above
Is more true to heaven
　　Than he to his love!

Will Nobody Marry Me?

Heigh-ho! for a husband!–Heigh-ho!
    There 's danger in longer delay!
Shall I never again have a beau?
    Will nobody marry me, pray!
I begin to feel strange, I declare!
    With beauty my prospects will fade–
I'd give myself up to despair
    If I thought I should die an old maid!

I once cut the beaux in a huff–
    I thought it a sin and a shame
That no one had spirit enough
    To ask me to alter my name.
So I turned up my nose at the short,
    And cast down my eyes at the tall;
But then I just did it in sport–
    And now I 've no lover at all!

These men are the plague of my life:
    'Tis hard from so many to choose!
Should any one wish for a wife,
    Could I have the heart to refuse?
I don't know–for none have proposed–
    Oh, dear me!–I'm frightened, I vow!
Good gracious! who ever supposed
    That I should be single till now?

EDWARD COOTE PINKNEY
(1802–1828)

Song

WE break the glass, whose sacred wine
  To some beloved health we drain,
Lest future pledges, less divine,
  Should e'er the hallowed toy profane;
And thus I broke a heart, that poured
  Its tide of feelings out for thee,
In draughts, by after-times deplored,
  Yet dear to memory.

But still the old, empassioned ways
  And habits of my mind remain,
And still unhappy light displays
  Thine image chambered in my brain,
And still it looks as when the hours
  Went by like flights of singing birds,
Or that soft chain of spoken flowers,
  And airy gems, thy words.

A Serenade

LOOK out upon the stars, my love,
    And shame them with thine eyes,
On which, than on the lights above,
    There hang more destinies.
Night's beauty is the harmony
    Of blending shades and light;
Then, Lady, up,—look out, and be
    A sister to the night!—

Sleep not!—thine image wakes for aye,
    Within my watching breast:
Sleep not!—from her soft sleep should fly,
    Who robs all hearts of rest.
Nay, Lady, from thy slumbers break,
    And make this darkness gay,
With looks, whose brightness well might make
    Of darker nights a day.

RALPH WALDO EMERSON
(1803–1882)

Give All to Love

GIVE all to love;
Obey thy heart;
Friends, kindred, days,
Estate, good fame,
Plans, credit, and the Muse—
Nothing refuse.

'Tis a brave master;
Let it have scope:
Follow it utterly,
Hope beyond hope:
High and more high
It dives into noon,
With wing unspent,
Untold intent;
But it is a god,
Knows its own path,
And the outlets of the sky.

It was never for the mean;
It requireth courage stout.
Souls above doubt,
Valor unbending,
It will reward, –
They shall return
More than they were,
And ever ascending.

Leave all for love;
Yet, hear me, yet,
One word more thy heart behoved,
One pulse more of firm endeavour, —
Keep thee to-day,
To-morrow, forever,
Free as an Arab
Of thy beloved.

Cling with life to the maid;
But when the surprise,
First vague shadow of surmise,
Flits across her bosom young,
Of a joy apart from thee,
Free be she, fancy-free;
Nor thou detain her vesture's hem,
Nor the palest rose she flung
From her summer diadem.

Though thou loved her as thyself,
As a self of purer clay;
Though her parting dims the day,
Stealing grace from all alive;
Heartily know,
When half-gods go
The gods arrive.

To Eva

O FAIR and stately maid, whose eyes
Were kindled in the upper skies
    At the same torch that lighted mine;
For so I must interpret still
Thy sweet dominion o'er my will,
    A sympathy divine.

Ah! let me blameless gaze upon
Features that seem at heart my own;
    Nor fear those watchful sentinels,
Who charm the more their glance forbids,
Chaste-glowing, underneath their lids,
    With fire that draws while it repels.

ELIZABETH BARRETT BROWNING
(1806–1861)

From: "Sonnets from the Portuguese"

If Thou Must Love Me

Sonnet XIV

IF thou must love me, let it be for nought
Except for love's sake only. Do not say
'I love her for her smile – her look – her way
Of speaking gently, – for a trick of thought
That falls in well with mine, and certes brought
A sense of pleasant ease on such a day'–
For these things in themselves, Belovèd, may
Be changed, or change for thee,–and love, so wrought,
May be unwrought so. Neither love me for
Thine own dear pity's wiping my cheeks dry,–
A creature might forget to weep, who bore
Thy comfort long, and lose thy love thereby!
But love me for love's sake, that evermore
Thou may'st love on, through love's eternity.

From: "Sonnets from the Portuguese"

Say Over Again, and Yet Once Over Again

Sonnet XXI

SAY over again, and yet once over again,
That thou dost love me. Though the word repeated
Should seem 'a cuckoo-song,' as thou dost treat it,
Remember, never to the hill or plain,
Valley and wood, without her cuckoo-strain
Comes the fresh Spring in all her green completed.
Belovèd, I, amid the darkness greeted
By a doubtful spirit-voice, in that doubt's pain
Cry, 'Speak once more—thou lovest!' Who can fear
Too many stars, though each in heaven shall roll,
Too many flowers, though each shall crown the year?
Say thou dost love me, love me, love me – toll
The silver iterance! – only minding, Dear,
To love me also in silence with thy soul.

From: "Sonnets from the Portuguese"

The First Time That The Sun Rose On Thine Oath

Sonnet XXXII

THE first time that the sun rose on thine oath
To love me, I looked forward to the moon
To slacken all those bonds which seemed too soon
And quickly tied to make a lasting troth.
Quick-loving hearts, I thought, may quickly loathe;
And, looking on myself, I seemed not one
For such man's love! – more like an out-of-tune
Worn viol, a good singer would be wroth
To spoil his song with, and which, snatched in haste,
Is laid down at the first ill-sounding note.
I did not wrong myself so, but I placed
A wrong on *thee*. For perfect strains may float
'Neath master-hands, from instruments defaced, –
And great souls, at one stroke, may do and doat.

From: "Sonnets from the Portuguese"

If I Leave All for Thee

Sonnet XXXV

IF I leave all for thee, wilt thou exchange
And be all to me? Shall I never miss
Home-talk and blessing and the common kiss
That comes to each in turn, nor count it strange,
When I look up, to drop on a new range
Of walls and floors, another home than this?
Nay, wilt thou fill that place by me which is
Filled by dead eyes too tender to know change?
That's hardest. If to conquer love, has tried,
To conquer grief, tries more, as all things prove;
For grief indeed is love and grief beside.
Alas, I have grieved so I am hard to love.
Yet love me—wilt thou? Open thine heart wide,
And fold within, the wet wings of thy dove.

From: "Sonnets from the Portuguese"

How Do I Love Thee?

Sonnet XLIII

HOW do I love thee? Let me count the ways.
I love thee to the depth and breadth and height
My soul can reach, when feeling out of sight
For the ends of Being and ideal Grace.
I love thee to the level of everyday's
Most quiet need, by sun and candlelight.
I love thee freely, as men strive for Right;
I love thee purely, as they turn from Praise.
I love thee with the passion put to use
In my old griefs, and with my childhood's faith.
I love thee with a love I seemed to lose
With my lost saints,— I love thee with the breath,
Smiles, tears, of all my life! — and, if God choose,
I shall but love thee better after death.

The Lady's Yes

'YES !' I answered you last night ;
   'No !' this morning, sir, I say:
Colours, seen by candle-light,
   Will not look the same by day.

When the tabors played their best,
   Lamps above, and laughs below ,
Love me sounded like a jest,
   Fit for *yes* or fit for *no*!

Call me false, or call me free,
   Vow, whatever light may shine, –
No man on your face shall see
   Any grief for change on mine.

Yet the sin is on us both;
   Time to dance is not to woo;
Wooer light makes fickle troth,
   Scorn of me recoils on *you*.

Learn to win a lady's faith
   Nobly, as the thing is high ,
Bravely, as for life and death,
   With a loyal gravity.

Lead her from the festive boards,
   Point her to the starry skies;
Guard her, by your truthful words,
   Pure from courtship's flatteries.

By your truth she shall be true,
   Ever true, as wives of yore;
And her *yes*, once said to you,
   SHALL be Yes for evermore.

A Denial

I

WE have met late—it is too late to meet,
    O friend, not more than friend!
Death's forecome shroud is tangled round my feet,
And if I step or stir, I touch the end.
    In this last jeopardy
Can I approach thee, I, who cannot move?
How shall I answer thy request for love?
    Look in my face and see.

II

I love thee not, I dare not love thee! go
    In silence; drop my hand.
If thou seek roses, seek them where they blow
In garden-alleys, not in desert-sand.
    Can life and death agree,
That thou shouldst stoop thy song to my complaint?
I cannot love thee. If the word is faint,
    Look in my face and see.

III

I might have loved thee in some former days.
    Oh, then, my spirits had leapt
As now they sink, at hearing thy love-praise!
Before these faded cheeks were overwept,
    Had this been asked of me,
To love thee with my whole strong heart and head,—
I should have said still ... yes, but smiled and said,
    "Look in my face and see!"

IV

But now ... God sees me, God, who took my heart
    And drowned it in life's surge.
In all your wide warm earth I have no part —

A light song overcomes me like a dirge.
    Could Love's great harmony
The saints keep step to when their bonds are loose,
Not weigh me down? am I a wife to choose?
    Look in my face and see —

V

While I behold, as plain as one who dreams,
    Some woman of full worth,
Whose voice, as cadenced as a silver stream's,
Shall prove the fountain-soul which sends it forth;
    One younger, more thought-free
And fair and gay, than I, thou must forget,
With brighter eyes than these . . . which are not wet . . .
    Look in my face and see!

VI

So farewell thou, whom I have known too late
    To let thee come so near.
Be counted happy while men call thee great,
And one belovèd woman feels thee dear! —
    Not I! — that cannot be.
I am lost, I am changed, — I must go farther, where
The change shall take me worse, and no one dare
    Look in my face and see.

VII

Meantime I bless thee. By these thoughts of mine
    I bless thee from all such!
I bless thy lamp to oil, thy cup to wine,
Thy hearth to joy, thy hand to an equal touch
    Of loyal troth. For me,
I love thee not, I love thee not! — away!
Here's no more courage in my soul to say
    'Look in my face and see.'

EDGAR ALLEN POE
(1809-1849)

A Valentine: To —— —— ——

FOR her this rhyme is penned, whose luminous eyes,
    Brightly expressive as the twins of Leda,
Shall find her own sweet name, that, nestling lies
    Upon the page, enwrapped from every reader.
Search narrowly the lines!– they hold a treasure
    Divine– a talisman– an amulet
That must be worn at heart. Search well the measure–
The words– the syllables! Do not forget
    The trivialest point, or you may lose your labor!
And yet there is in this no Gordian knot
    Which one might not undo without a sabre,
If one could merely comprehend the plot.
    Enwritten upon the leaf where now are peering
Eyes scintillating soul, there lies perdus
    Three eloquent words oft uttered in the hearing
Of poets, by poets– as the name is a poet's, too.
    Its letters, although naturally lying
Like the knight Pinto– Mendez Ferdinando–
    Still form a synonym for Truth.– Cease trying!
You will not read the riddle, though you do the best you can do.

HENRY WADSWORTH LONGFELLOW
(1807–1882)

Maidenhood

MAIDEN! with the meek, brown eyes,
In whose orbs a shadow lies
Like the dusk in evening skies!

Thou whose locks outshine the sun,
Golden tresses, wreathed in one,
As the braided streamlets run!

Standing, with reluctant feet,
Where the brook and river meet,
Womanhood and childhood fleet!

Gazing, with a timid glance,
On the brooklet's swift advance,
On the river's broad expanse!

Deep and still, that gliding stream
Beautiful to thee must seem,
As the river of a dream.

Then why pause with indecision,
When bright angels in thy vision
Beckon thee to fields Elysian?

Seest thou shadows sailing by,
As the dove, with startled eye
Sees the falcon's shadow fly?

Hearest thou voices on the shore,
That our ears perceive no more,
Deafened by the cataract's roar?

Oh, thou child of many prayers!
Life hath quicksands, Life hath snares!
Care and age come unawares!

Like the swell of some sweet tune
Morning rises into noon,
May glides onward into June.

Childhood is the bough, where slumbered
Birds and blossoms many-numbered;—
Age, that bough with snows encumbered.

Gather, then, each flower that grows,
When the young heart overflows,
To embalm that tent of snows.

Bear a lily in thy hand;
Gates of brass cannot withstand
One touch of that magic wand.

Bear through sorrow, wrong, and truth
In thy heart the dew of youth,
On thy lips the smile of truth.

O, that dew, like balm, shall steal
Into wounds, that cannot heal
Even as sleep our eyes doth seal;

And that smile, like sunshine, dart
Into many a sunless heart,
For a smile of God thou art.

Endymion

The rising moon has hid the stars;
Her level rays, like golden bars,
    Lie on the landscape green,
    With shadows brown between.

And silver white the river gleams,
As if Diana, in her dreams,
    Had dropt her silver bow
    Upon the meadows low.

On such a tranquil night as this,
She woke Endymion with a kiss,
    When, sleeping in the grove,
    He dreamed not of her love.

Like Dian's kiss, unasked, unsought,
Love gives itself, but is not bought;
    Nor voice, nor sound betrays
    Its deep, impassioned gaze.

It comes,—the beautiful, the free,
The crown of all humanity,—
    In silence and alone
    To seek the elected one.

It lifts the boughs, whose shadows deep
Are Life's oblivion, the soul's sleep,
    And kisses the closed eyes
    Of him who slumbering lies.

O weary hearts! O slumbering eyes!
O drooping souls, whose destinies
    Are fraught with fear and pain,
    Ye shall be loved again!

No one is so accursed by fate,
No one so utterly desolate,
But some heart, though unknown,
Responds unto his own.

Responds,— as if with unseen wings,
An angel touched its quivering strings;
And whispers, in its song,
"Where hast thou stayed so long?"

Song

Where, from the eye of the day,
    The dark and silent river
Pursues through tangled woods a way
    O'er which the tall trees quiver;

The silver mist, that breaks
    From out that woodland cover,
Betrays the hidden path it takes,
    And hangs the current over!

So oft the thoughts that burst
    From hidden springs of feeling,
Like silent streams, unseen at first,
    From our cold hearts are stealing:

But soon the clouds that veil
    The eye of Love, when glowing,
Betray the long unwhispered tale
    Of thoughts in darkness flowing!

ALFRED, LORD TENNYSON
(1809-1892)

Summer Night

NOW sleeps the crimson petal, now the white;
Nor waves the cypress in the palace walk;
Nor winks the gold fin in the porphyry font:
The firefly wakens: waken thou with me.

Now droops the milk-white peacock like a ghost,
And like a ghost she glimmers on to me.

Now lies the Earth all Danaë to the stars,
And all thy heart lies open unto me.

Now slides the silent meteor on, and leaves
A shining furrow, as thy thoughts in me.

Now folds the lily all her sweetness up,
And slips into the bosom of the lake:
So fold thyself, my dearest, thou, and slip
Into my bosom and be lost in me.

At The Window

Vine, vine and eglantine,
Clasp her window, trail and twine!
Rose, rose and clematis,
Trail and twine and clasp and kiss,
Kiss, kiss; and make her a bower
    All of flowers, and drop me a flower,
      Drop me a flower.

Vine, vine and eglantine,
Cannot a flower, a flower, be mine?
Rose, rose and clematis,
Drop me a flower, a flower, to kiss,
Kiss, kiss – and out of her bower
    All of flowers, a flower, a flower,
      Dropt, a flower.

Marriage Morning

Light, so low upon earth,
    You send a flash to the sun.
Here is the golden close of love,
    All my wooing is done.
Oh, the woods and the meadows,
    Woods where we hid from the wet,
Stiles where we stay'd to be kind,
    Meadows in which we met!
Light, so low in the vale
    You flash and lighten afar,
For this is the golden morning of love,
    And you are his morning star.
Flash, I am coming, I come,
    By meadow and stile and wood,
Oh, lighten into my eyes and my heart,
    Into my heart and my blood!
Heart, are you great enough
    For a love that never tires?
O heart, are you great enough for love?
    I have heard of thorns and briers.
Over the thorns and briers,
    Over the meadows and stiles,
Over the world to the end of it
    Flash for a million miles.

OLIVER WENDELL HOLMES
(1809–1894)

The Philosopher to His Love

DEAREST, a look is but a ray
Reflected in a certain way;
A word, whatever tone it wear,
Is but a trembling wave of air;
A touch, obedience to a clause
In nature's pure material laws.

The very flowers that bend and meet,
In sweetening others, grow more sweet;
The clouds by day, the stars by night,
Inweave their floating locks of light;
The rainbow, Heaven's own forehead's braid,
Is but the embrace of sun and shade.

How few that love us have we found!
How wide the world that girds them round!
Like mountain streams we meet and part,
Each living in the other's heart,
Our course unknown, our hope to be
Yet mingled in the distant sea.

But Ocean coils and heaves in vain,
Bound in the subtle moonbeam's chain;
And love and hope do but obey
Some cold, capricious planet's ray,
Which lights and leads the tide it charms
To Death's dark caves and icy arms.

Alas! one narrow line is drawn,
That links our sunset with our dawn;
In mist and shade life's morning rose,
And clouds are round it at its close;
But ah! no twilight beam ascends
To whisper where that evening ends.

Oh! in the hour when I shall feel
Those shadows round my senses steal,
When gentle eyes are weeping o'er
The clay that feels their tears no more,
Then let thy spirit with me be,
Or some sweet angel, likest thee!

ROBERT BROWNING
(1812–1889)

Life in a Love

ESCAPE me?
Never –
Beloved!
While I am I, and you are you,
　So long as the world contains us both,
　Me the loving and you the loth,
While the one eludes, must the other pursue.
My life is a fault at last, I fear:
　It seems too much like a fate, indeed!
　Though I do my best I shall scarce succeed.
But what if I fail of my purpose here?
It is but to keep the nerves at strain,
　To dry one's eyes and laugh at a fall,
And, baffled, get up and begin again,–
　So the chace takes up one's life, that's all.
While, look but once from your farthest bound
　At me so deep in the dust and dark,
No sooner the old hope goes to ground
　Than a new one, straight to the self-same mark,
　　I shape me –
　　Ever
　　Removed!

Love in a Life

ROOM after room,
I hunt the house through
We inhabit together.
Heart, fear nothing, for, heart, thou shalt find her –
Next time, herself! – not the trouble behind her
Left in the curtain, the couch's perfume!
As she brushed it, the cornice-wreath blossomed anew:
Yon looking-glass gleamed at the wave of her feather.

Yet the day wears,
And door succeeds door;
I try the fresh fortune –
Range the wide house from the wing to the centre.
Still the same chance! she goes out as I enter.
Spend my whole day in the quest, – who cares?
But 'tis twilight, you see,– with such suites to explore,
Such closets to search, such alcoves to importune!

My Star

ALL that I know
    Of a certain star,
Is, it can throw
    (Like the angled spar)
Now a dart of red,
    Now a dart of blue;
Till my friends have said
    They would fain see, too,
My star that dartles the red and the blue!
Then it stops like a bird; like a flower, hangs furled:
    They must solace themselves with the Saturn above
    it.
What matter to me if their star is a world?
    Mine has opened its soul to me; therefore I love it.

Meeting at Night

THE gray sea and the long black land;
And the yellow half-moon large and low;
And the startled little waves that leap
In fiery ringlets from their sleep,
As I gain the cove with pushing prow,
And quench its speed i' the slushy sand.

Then a mile of warm sea-scented beach;
Three fields to cross till a farm appears;
A tap at the pane, the quick sharp scratch
And blue spurt of a lighted match,
And a voice less loud, thro' its joys and fears,
Than the two hearts beating each to each!

You'll Love Me Yet

From: "Pippa Passes"

YOU'LL love me yet! – and I can tarry
    Your love's protracted growing:
June rear'd that bunch of flowers you carry,
    From seeds of April's sowing.

I plant a heartful now: some seed
    At least is sure to strike,
And yield – what you'll not pluck indeed,
    Not love, but, may be, like.

You'll look at least on love's remains,
    A grave 's one violet:
Your look? – that pays a thousand pains.
    What 's death?   You'll love me yet!

JAMES RUSSELL LOWELL
(1819-1891)

A Valentine

LET others wonder what fair face
    Upon their path shall shine,
And, fancying half, half hoping, trace
    Some maiden shape of tenderest grace
        To be their Valentine.

Let other hearts with tremor sweet
    One secret wish enshrine
That Fate may lead their happy feet
    Fair Julia in the lane to meet
        To be their Valentine.

But I, far happier, am secure;
    I know the eyes benign,
The face more beautiful and pure
    Than Fancy's fairest portraiture
        That mark my Valentine.

More than when first I singled thee,
    This only prayer is mine,—
That, in the years I yet shall see,
    As, darling, in the past, thou 'lt be
        My happy Valentine.

The Nobler Lover

IF he be a nobler lover, take him!
    You in you I seek, and not myself;
Love with men 's what women choose to make him,
    Seraph strong to soar, or fawn-eyed elf:
All I am or can, your beauty gave it,
    Lifting me a moment nigh to you,
And my bit of heaven, I fain would save it—
    Mine I thought it was, I never knew.

What you take of me is yours to serve you,
    All I give, you gave to me before;
Let him win you! If I but deserve you,
    I keep all you grant to him and more:
You shall make me dare what others dare not,
    You shall keep my nature pure as snow,
And a light from you that others share not
    Shall transfigure me where'er I go.

Let me be your thrall! However lowly
    Be the bondsman's service I can do,
Loyalty shall make it high and holy;
    Naught can be unworthy, done for you.
Men shall say, "A lover of this fashion
    Such an icy mistress well beseems."
Women say, "Could we deserve such passion,
    We might be the marvel that he dreams."

WALT WHITMAN
(1819-1892)

Are You the New Person Drawn Toward Me?

ARE you the new person drawn toward me?
To begin with, take warning–I am surely far different
   from what you suppose;
Do you suppose you will find in me your ideal?
Do you think it so easy to have me become your lover?
Do you think the friendship of me would be unalloy'd
   satisfaction?
Do you think I am trusty and faithful?
Do you see no further than this façade–this smooth and
   tolerant manner of me?
Do you suppose yourself advancing on real ground
   toward a real heroic man?
Have you no thought, O dreamer, that it may be all
   maya, illusion?

Among The Multitude

1

AMONG the men and women, the multitude,
I perceive one picking me out by secret and divine
    signs,
Acknowledging none else—not parent, wife, husband,
    brother, child, any nearer than I am;
Some are baffled—But that one is not—that one knows
    me.

2

Ah, lover and perfect equal!
I meant that you should discover me so, by my faint
    indirections;
And I, when I meet you, mean to discover you by the
    like in you.

HENRY HOWARD BROWNELL
(1820-1872)

To M—.

THEY told me thou wert beautiful – that on thy fair young face,
A poet's wish, a lover's dream might find their resting-place.
And well indeed the bud that bloomed so bright in early Spring,
Bore promise of a fairer flower, that summer suns would bring –
Yet not so sweet in form and hue, all unprofaned by art,
(Though these alone might well suffice to move the coldest
    heart,)
As that, in goodness – gentleness – and purity alone,
'Tis radiant as the angels' are, before the Eternal Throne.
Long have I cherished Loveliness – yet never knew till now,
How deeply this adoring heart before its shrine could bow.

And they said thy voice was music–and that I knew full well –
Though years had passed, since on my heart its gentle accents fell!
That voice, to whose endearing tones I listened long before,
And, having heard those accents once, could never lose it more.
'Twas like some old forgotten song, yet once to memory dear –
Some long-lost strain of music, familiar to mine ear.
And as its tones were heard once more, what nameless thoughts
    were stirred–
What memories from their slumber awoke at every word–
What tender visions once again across Life's desert stole,
And Hopes and Fears, a countless throng, came mingling o'er the
    soul.

And yet I cannot envy him, who ne'er hath felt the same;
Whose heart has thrilled not at the sound of one beloved Name;
Whose pulse hath never quickened at the footstep, or the tone
Of one, whose every hope and thought are dearer than his own:
Or never felt, as now I feel, that all once wildly sought
Has yielded to one gentle hope – one dear entrancing thought:
That one sweet glance of kindness from those dear eyes of light,
Could ransom all the dreary Past, and make the Future bright,
To him whose only happiness, – whose only refuge lies
In the calm soul-lit heaven of those beloved eyes.

To S—.

A STRANGER came – a stranger met –
   They parted, and for aye –
Yet one, perchance, remembers yet
   Those moments passed away.
They woke a vision sweet and vain,
He never thought to dream again.

As yon lone cloud, whose passing shade
   Floats on the summer wind –
Soon from the sun-lit heaven shall fade,
   And leave no trace behind –
Thus, in the hour that bade them part,
His memory vanished from her heart.

So be it still – the days are past
   Of reckless, wild desire;
Yet must he cherish to the last,
   And love – what all admire –
And bear, through sunshine and through storm,
That gentle heart, and lovely form.

A Woman's Poem

YOU say you love me, and you lay
    Your hand and fortune at my feet:
I thank you, sir, with all my heart,
        For love is sweet.

It is but little to you men,
    To whom the doors of Life stand wide;
But much, how much to woman! She
        Has naught beside.

You make the worlds wherein you move,
    You rule your tastes, or coarse, or fine;
Dine, hunt, or fish, or waste your gold
        At dice and wine.

Our world (alas, you make that, too!)
    Is narrower, shut in four blank walls:
Know you, or care, what light is there?
        What shadow falls?

We read the last new novel out,
    And live in dream-land till it ends:
We write romantic school-girl notes,
        That bore our friends.

We learn to trill Italian songs,
    And thrum for hours the tortured keys:
We think it pleases you, and we
        But live to please.

We feed our birds, we tend our flowers,
    (Poor in-door things of sickly bloom,)
Or play the housewife in our gloves,
        And dust the room.

But some of us have hearts and minds,
     So much the worse for us and you;
For grant we seek a better life,
          What can we do?

We cannot build and sail your ships,
     Or drive your engines; we are weak,
And ignorant of the tricks of Trade.
          To think, and speak,

Or write some earnest, stammering words
     Alone is ours, and that you hate;
So forced within ourselves again
          We sigh and wait.

Ah, who can tell the bitter hours,
     The dreary days, that women spend?
Their thoughts unshared, their lives unknown,
          Without a friend!

Without a friend? And what is he,
     Who, like a shadow, day and night,
Follows the woman he prefers—
          Lives in her sight?

Her lover, he: a gallant man,
     Devoted to her every whim;
He vows to die for her, so she
          Must live for him!

We should be very grateful, sir,
     That, when you 've nothing else to do,
You waste your idle hours on us—
          So kind of you!

Profuse in studied compliments,
     Your manners like your clothes are fine,
Though both at times are somewhat strong
          Of smoke and wine.

What can we hope to know of you?
    Or you of us? We act our parts:
We love in jest: it is the play
    Of hands, not hearts!

You grant my bitter words are true
    Of others, not of you and me;
Your love is steady as a star:
    But we shall see.

You say you love me: have you thought
    How much those little words contain?
Alas, a world of happiness,
    And worlds of pain!

You know, or should, your nature now,
    Its needs and passions. Can I be
What you desire me? Do you find
    Your all in me?

You do. But have you thought that I
    May have my ways and fancies, too?
You love me well; but have you thought
    If I love you?

But think again. You know me not:
    I, too, may be a butterfly,
A costly parlor doll on show
    For you to buy.

You trust me wholly? One word more.
    You see me young: they call me fair:
I think I have a pleasant face,
    And pretty hair.

But by and by my face will fade,
    It must with time, it may with care:
What say you to a wrinkled wife,
    With thin, gray hair?

You care not, you: in youth, or age,
　　Your heart is mine, while life endures.
Is it so? Then, Arthur, here 's my hand,
　　My heart is yours.

DANTE GABRIEL ROSSETTI
(1828-1882)

The Kiss

WHAT smouldering senses in death's sick delay
    Or seizure of malign vicissitude
    Can rob this body of honour, or denude
This soul of wedding-raiment worn to-day?
For lo! even now my lady's lips did play
    With these my lips such consonant interlude
    As laurelled Orpheus longed for when he wooed
The half-drawn hungering face with that last lay.

I was a child beneath her touch, — a man
    When breast to breast we clung, even I and she,
    A spirit when her spirit looked through me, –
A god when all our life-breath met to fan
Our life-blood, till love's emulous ardours ran,
    Fire within fire, desire in deity.

Genius in Beauty

BEAUTY like hers is genius. Not the call
    Of Homer's or of Dante's heart sublime, –
    Not Michael's hand furrowing the zones of time, –
Is more with compassed mysteries musical;
Nay, not in Spring's or Summer's sweet footfall
    More gathered gifts exuberant Life bequeaths
    Than doth this sovereign face, whose love-spell
    breathes

Even from its shadowed contour on the wall.
As many men are poets in their youth,
    But for one sweet-strung soul the wires prolong
    Even through all change the indomitable song;
So in likewise the envenomed years, whose tooth
Rends shallower grace with ruin void of truth,
    Upon this beauty's power shall wreak no wrong.

Silent Noon

YOUR hands lie open in the long fresh grass,–
    The finger-points look through like rosy blooms:
    Your eyes smile peace. The pasture gleams and
    glooms
'Neath billowing skies that scatter and amass.
All round our nest, far as the eye can pass,
    Are golden kingcup-fields with silver edge
    Where the cow-parsley skirts the hawthorn-hedge.
'Tis visible silence, still as the hour-glass.

Deep in the sun-search'd growths the dragon-fly
Hangs like a blue thread loosen'd from the sky:–
    So this wing'd hour is dropt to us from above.
Oh! clasp we to our hearts, for deathless dower,
This close-companion'd inarticulate hour
    When twofold silence was the song of love.

Insomnia

THIN are the night-skirts left behind
   By daybreak hours that onward creep,
    And thin, alas! the shred of sleep
That wavers with the spirit's wind:
But in half-dreams that shift and roll
  And still remember and forget,
My soul this hour has drawn your soul
    A little nearer yet.

Our lives, most dear, are never near,
   Our thoughts are never far apart,
    Though all that draws us heart to heart
Seems fainter now and now more clear.
To-night Love claims his full control,
   And with desire and with regret
My soul this hour has drawn your soul
    A little nearer yet.

Is there a home where heavy earth
   Melts to bright air that breathes no pain,
    Where water leaves no thirst again
And springing fire is Love's new birth?
If faith long bound to one true goal
   May there at length its hope beget,
My soul that hour shall draw your soul
    For ever nearer yet.

Youth's Antiphony

"I LOVE you, sweet: how can you ever learn
    How much I love you?" "You I love even so,
    And so I learn it." "Sweet, you cannot know
How fair you are." "If fair enough to earn
Your love, so much is all my love's concern."
    "My love grows hourly, sweet." "Mine too doth
    grow,
    Yet love seemed full so many hours ago!"
Thus lovers speak, till kisses claim their turn.

Ah! happy they to whom such words as these
    In youth have served for speech the whole day
    long,
    Hour after hour, remote from the world's throng,
Work, contest, fame, all life's confederate pleas,—
What while Love breathed in sighs and silences
    Through two blent souls one rapturous undersong.

CHRISTINA GEORGINA ROSSETTI
(1830–1894)

Remember

REMEMBER me when I am gone away,
    Gone far away into the silent land;
    When you can no more hold me by the hand,
Nor I half turn to go yet turning stay.
Remember me when no more day by day
    You tell me of our future that you planned:
    Only remember me; you understand
It will be late to counsel then or pray.
Yet if you should forget me for a while
    And afterwards remember, do not grieve:
    For if the darkness and corruption leave
    A vestige of the thoughts that once I had,
Better by far you should forget and smile
    Than that you should remember and be sad.

Monna Insominata: A Sonnet of Sonnets

1

Lo dì che han detto a' dolci amici addio.   *(Dante)*
Amor, con quanto sforzo oggi mi vinci!   *(Petrarca)*

COME back to me, who wait and watch for you:—
    Or come not yet, for it is over then,
    And long it is before you come again,
So far between my pleasures are and few.
While, when you come not, what I do I do
    Thinking "Now when he comes," my sweetest
    "when:"
    For one man is my world of all the men
This wide world holds; O love, my world is you.
Howbeit, to meet you grows almost a pang
    Because the pang of parting comes so soon;
    My hope hangs waning, waxing, like a moon
    Between the heavenly days on which we meet:
Ah me, but where are now the songs I sang
    When life was sweet because you call'd them
    sweet?

Era già 1'ora che volge il desio.   *(Dante)*
Ricorro al tempo ch' io vi vidi prima.   *(Petrarca)*

I WISH I could remember that first day,
    First hour, first moment of your meeting me,
    If bright or dim the season, it might be
Summer or winter for aught I can say;
So unrecorded did it slip away,
    So blind was I to see and to foresee,
    So dull to mark the budding of my tree
That would not blossom yet for many a May.
If only I could recollect it, such
    A day of days! I let it come and go
    As traceless as a thaw of bygone snow;
    It seem'd to mean so little, meant so much;
If only now I could recall that touch,
    First touch of hand in hand—Did one but know!

3

O ombre vane, fuor che ne l'aspetto! (Dante)
Immaginata guida la conduce. (Petrarca)

I DREAM of you to wake: would that I might
    Dream of you and not wake but slumber on;
    Nor find with dreams the dear companion gone,
As Summer ended Summer birds take flight.
In happy dreams I hold you full in sight,
    I blush again who waking look so wan;
    Brighter than sunniest day that ever shone,
In happy dreams your smile makes day of night.
Thus only in a dream we are at one,
    Thus only in a dream we give and take
The faith that maketh rich who take or give;
    If thus to sleep is sweeter than to wake,
To die were surely sweeter than to live,
    Though there be nothing new beneath the sun.

4

Poca favilla gran fliamma seconda.   *(Dante)*

Ogni altra cosa, ogni pensier va fore,
E sol ivi con voi rimansi amore.   *(Petrarca)*

I LOVED you first: but afterwards your love
    Outsoaring mine, sang such a loftier song
As drowned the friendly cooings of my dove.
      Which owes the other most? my love was long,
      And yours one moment seemed to wax more
        strong;
I loved and guessed at you, you construed me—
And loved me for what might or might not be—
      Nay, weights and measures do us both a wrong.
For verily love knows not "mine" or "thine;"
      With separate "I" and "thou" free love has done,
        For one is both and both are one in love:
Rich love knows nought of "thine that is not mine;"
      Both have the strength and both the length
        thereof,
    Both of us of the love which makes us one.

Amor che a nullo amato amar perdona.　　　　　*(Dante)*
Amor m'addusse in sì gioiosa spene.　　　　　*(Petrarca)*

O MY heart's heart, and you who are to me
　　　More than myself myself, God be with you,
　　　Keep you in strong obedience leal and true
To Him whose noble service setteth free,
Give you all good we see or can foresee,
　　　Make your joys many and your sorrows few,
　　　Bless you in what you bear and what you do,
Yea, perfect you as He would have you be.
So much for you; but what for me, dear friend?
　　　To love you without stint and all I can
Today, tomorrow, world without an end;
　　　To love you much and yet to love you more,
　　　As Jordan at his flood sweeps either shore;
Since woman is the helpmeet made for man.

Or puoi la quantitate
Comprender de l'amor che a te mi scalda.   *(Dante)*
Non vo' che da tal nodo mi scioglia.   *(Petrarca)*

TRUST me, I have not earned your dear rebuke,
    I love, as you would have me, God the most;
      Would lose not Him, but you, must one be lost,
Nor with Lot's wife cast back a faithless look
Unready to forego what I forsook;
    This say I, having counted up the cost,
      This, though I be the feeblest of God's host,
The sorriest sheep Christ shepherds with His crook.
Yet while I love my God the most, I deem
    That I can never love you overmuch;
      I love Him more, so let me love you too;
    Yea, as I apprehend it, love is such
I cannot love you if I love not Him,
      I cannot love Him if I love not you.

Qui primavera sempre ed ogni frutto.   *(Dante)*
Ragionando con meco ed io con lui.   *(Petrarca)*

"LOVE me, for I love you"—and answer me,
  "Love me, for I love you"—so shall we stand
  As happy equals in the flowering land
Of love, that knows not a dividing sea.
Love builds the house on rock and not on sand,
  Love laughs what while the winds rave desperately;
And who hath found love's citadel unmanned?
  And who hath held in bonds love's liberty?
My heart's a coward though my words are brave—
  We meet so seldom, yet we surely part
  So often; there's a problem for your art!
   Still I find comfort in his Book, who saith,
Though jealousy be cruel as the grave,
  And death be strong, yet love is strong as death.

Come dicesse a Dio: D'altro non calme.   *(Dante)*
Spero trovar pietà non che perdono.   *(Petrarca)*

"I, IF I perish, perish"—Esther spake:
    And bride of life or death she made her fair
    In all the lustre of her perfumed hair
And smiles that kindle longing but to slake.
She put on pomp of loveliness, to take
    Her husband through his eyes at unaware;
    She spread abroad her beauty for a snare,
Harmless as doves and subtle as a snake.
She trapped him with one mesh of silken hair,
    She vanquished him by wisdom of her wit,
        And built her people's house that it should
        stand:—
        If I might take my life so in my hand,
And for my love to Love put up my prayer,
    And for love's sake by Love be granted it!

O dignitosa coscienza e netta!   *(Dante)*
Spirto più acceso di virtuti ardenti.   *(Petrarca)*

THINKING of you, and all that was, and all
    That might have been and now can never be,
    I feel your honored excellence, and see
Myself unworthy of the happier call:
For woe is me who walk so apt to fall,
    So apt to shrink afraid, so apt to flee,
    Apt to lie down and die (ah, woe is me!)
Faithless and hopeless turning to the wall.
And yet not hopeless quite nor faithless quite,
Because not loveless; love may toil all night,
    But take at morning; wrestle till the break
        Of day, but then wield power with God and
        man:–
        So take I heart of grace as best I can,
    Ready to spend and be spent for your sake.

Con miglior corso e con migliore stella.   *(Dante)*
La vita fugge e non s'arresta un' ora.   *(Petrarca)*

TIME flies, hope flags, life plies a wearied wing;
    Death following hard on life gains ground apace;
    Faith runs with each and rears an eager face,
Outruns the rest, makes light of everything,
Spurns earth, and still finds breath to pray and sing;
    While love ahead of all uplifts his praise,
    Still asks for grace and still gives thanks for grace,
Content with all day brings and night will bring.
Life wanes; and when love folds his wings above
    Tired hope, and less we feel his conscious pulse,
      Let us go fall asleep, dear friend, in peace:
      A little while, and age and sorrow cease;
    A little while, and life reborn annuls
Loss and decay and death, and all is love.

Vien dietro a me e lascia dir le genti.   *(Dante)*
Contando i casi della vita nostra.   *(Petrarca)*

MANY in aftertimes will say of you
    "He loved her"—while of me what will they say?
    Not that I loved you more than just in play,
For fashion's sake as idle women do.
Even let them prate; who know not what we knew
    Of love and parting in exceeding pain,
    Of parting hopeless here to meet again,
Hopeless on earth, and heaven is out of view.
But by my heart of love laid bare to you,
    My love that you can make not void nor vain,
Love that foregoes you but to claim anew
        Beyond this passage of the gate of death,
    I charge you at the Judgment make it plain
        My love of you was life and not a breath.

Amor, che ne la mente mi ragiona. (Dante)
Amor vien nel bel viso di costei. (Petrarca)

IF there be any one can take my place
 And make you happy whom I grieve to grieve,
 Think not that I can grudge it, but believe
I do commend you to that nobler grace,
That readier wit than mine, that sweeter face;
 Yea, since your riches make me rich, conceive
 I too am crowned, while bridal crowns I weave,
And thread the bridal dance with jocund pace.
For if I did not love you, it might be
 That I should grudge you some one dear delight;
 But since the heart is yours that was mine own,
Your pleasure is my pleasure, right my right,
Your honourable freedom makes me free,
 And you companioned I am not alone.

E drizzeremo gli occhi al Primo Amore.　　　　(Dante)
Ma trovo peso non da le mie braccia.　　　　(Petrarca)

IF I could trust mine own self with your fate,
　　Shall I not rather trust it in God's hand?
　　Without Whose Will one lily doth not stand,
Nor sparrow fall at his appointed date;
　　Who numbereth the innumerable sand,
Who weighs the wind and water with a weight,
To Whom the world is neither small nor great,
　　Whose knowledge foreknew every plan we
　　planned.
Searching my heart for all that touches you,
　　I find there only love and love's goodwill
Helpless to help and impotent to do,
　　Of understanding dull, of sight most dim;
　　And therefore I commend you back to Him
Whose love your love's capacity can fill.

14

E la Sua Volontade è nostra pace. (Dante)
Sol con questi pensier, con altre chiome. (Petrarca)

YOUTH gone, and beauty gone if ever there
    Dwelt beauty in so poor a face as this;
      Youth gone and beauty, what remains of bliss?
I will not bind fresh roses in my hair,
To shame a cheek at best but little fair,–
    Leave youth his roses, who can bear a thorn,–
I will not seek for blossoms anywhere,
    Except such common flowers as blow with corn.
Youth gone and beauty gone, what doth remain?
    The longing of a heart pent up forlorn,
      A silent heart whose silence loves and longs;
      The silence of a heart which sang its songs
    While youth and beauty made a summer morn,
Silence of love that cannot sing again.

EMILY DICKINSON
(1830-1886)

Mine

MINE by the right of the white election!
Mine by the royal seal!
Mine by the sign in the scarlet prison
Bars cannot conceal!

Mine, here in vision and in veto!
Mine, by the grave's repeal
Titled, confirmed, – delirious charter!
Mine, while the ages steal!

Love's Humility

MY worthiness is all my doubt,
    His merit all my fear,
Constrasting which, my qualities
    Do lowlier appear;

Lest I should insufficient prove
    For his beloved need,
The chiefest apprehension
    Within my loving creed.

So I, the undivine abode
    Of his elect content,
Conform my soul as 't were a church
    Unto her sacrament.

Love

LOVE is anterior to life,
    Posterior to death,
Initial of creation, and
    The exponent of breath.

The Letter

"GOING to him! Happy letter! Tell him –
Tell him the page I didn't write;
Tell him I only said the syntax,
And left the verb and the pronoun out.
Tell him just how the fingers hurried,
Then how they waded, slow, slow, slow;
And then you wished you had eyes in your pages,
So you could see what moved them so.

"Tell him it wasn't a practised writer,
You guessed, from the way the sentence toiled;
You could hear the bodice tug, behind you,
As if it held but the might of a child;
You almost pitied it, you, it worked so.
Tell him – No, you may quibble there,
For it would split his heart to know it,
And then you and I were silenter.

"Tell him night finished before we finished,
And the old clock kept neighing 'day!'
And you got sleepy and begged to be ended –
What could it hinder so, to say?
Tell him just how she sealed you, cautious,
But if he ask where you are id
Until to-morrow, – happy letter!
Gesture, coquette, and shake your head!"

Proof

THAT I did always love,
I bring thee proof:
That till I loved
I did not love enough.

That I shall love alway,
I offer thee
That love is life,
And life hath immortality.

This, dost thou doubt, sweet?
Then have I
Nothing to show
But Cavalry.

Surrender

DOUBT me, my dim companion!
Why, God would be content
With but a fraction of the love
Poured thee without a stint.
The whole of me, forever,
What more the woman can, –
Say quick, that I may dower thee
With last delight I own!

It cannot be my spirit,
For that was thine before;
I ceded all of dust I knew, –
What opulence the more
Had I, a humble maiden,
Whose farthest of degree
Was that she might,
Some distant heaven,
Dwell timidly with thee!

Love's Baptism

I'M ceded, I've stopped being theirs;
The name they dropped upon my face
With water, in the country's church,
Is finished using now,
And they can put it with my dolls,
My childhood, and the string of spools
I've finished threading too.

Baptized before without the choice,
But this time consciously, of grace
Unto supremest name,
Called to my full, the crescent dropped,
Existence's whole are filled up
With one small diadem.

My second rank, too small the first,
Crowned, crowing on my father's breast,
A half unconscious queen;
But this time, adequate, erect,
With will to choose, or to reject,
And I choose – just a throne.

Wild Nights! Wild Nights!

WILD nights! Wild nights!
Were I with thee,
Wild nights should be
Our luxury!

Futile the winds
To a heart in port, –
Done with the compass,
Done with the chart.

Rowing in Eden!
Ah! the sea!
Might I but moor
To-night in thee!

The Lovers

THE rose did caper on her cheek,
Her bodice rose and fell,
Her pretty speech, like drunken men,
Did stagger pitiful.

Her fingers fumbled at her work, –
Her needle would not go;
What ailed so smart a little maid
It puzzled me to know,

Till opposite I spied a cheek
That bore another rose;
Just opposite another speech
That like the drunkard goes;

A vest that, like the bodice, danced
To the immortal tune, –
Till those two troubled little clocks
Ticked softly into one.

He Touched Me, So I Live to Know

HE touched me, so I live to know
That such a day, permitted so,
   I groped upon his breast.
It was a boundless place to me,
And silenced, as the awful sea
   Puts minor streams to rest.

And now, I'm different from before,
As if I breathed superior air,
   Or brushed a royal gown;
My feet, too, that had wandered so,
My gypsy face transfigured now
   To tenderer renown.

If I May Have It When It's Dead

IF I may have it when it's dead
    I will contented be;
If just as soon as breath is out
    It shall belong to me,

Until they lock it in the grave,
    'T is bliss I cannot weigh,
For though they lock thee in the grave,
    Myself can hold the key.

Think of it, lover! I and thee
    Permitted face to face to be;
After a life, a death we'll say,–
    For death was that, and this is thee.

HELEN HUNT JACKSON
(1830–1885)

Tryst

SOMEWHERE thou awaitest,
    And I, with lips unkissed,
Weep that thus to latest
    Thou puttest off our tryst!

The golden bowls are broken,
    The silver cords untwine;
Almond flowers in token
    Have bloomed,–that I am thine!

Others who would fly thee
    In cowardly alarms,
Who hate thee and deny thee,
    Thou foldest in thine arms!

How shall I entreat thee
    No longer to withhold?
I dare not go to meet thee,
    O lover, far and cold!

O lover, whose lips chilling
    So many lips have kissed,
Come, even if unwilling,
    And keep thy solemn tryst!

Love's Largess

AT my heart's door
Love standeth, like a king beside
His royal treasury, whose wide
Gates open swing, and cannot hide
    Their priceless store.

His touch and hold
Its common things to jewels turned;
In his sweet fires the dross he burned
Away; and thus he won and earned
    And made its gold.

So rich I find
Myself in service of this king,
The goods we spare, in alms I fling;
And breathless days too few hours bring
    Me to be kind.

To sould whose pain
My heart can scarcely dare to greet
With pity, while my own complete
And blessed joy their loss must mete
    By my great gain.

Diviner air
Of beauty, and a grace more free,
More soft and solemn depths I see
In every woman's face, since he
    Has called me fair.

WILLIAM MORRIS
(1834–1896)

From: "Love is Enough"

I

LOVE IS ENOUGH: though the World be a-waning
  And the woods have no voice but the voice of complaining,
  Though the sky be too dark for dim eyes to discover
The gold-cups and daisies fair blooming thereunder,
Though the hills be held shadows, and the sea a dark wonder,
  And this day draw a veil over all deeds passed over,
Yet their hands shall not tremble, their feet shall not falter;
The void shall not weary, the fear shall not alter
  These lips and these eyes of the loved and the lover.

LOVE IS ENOUGH: have no thought for to-morrow
If ye lie down this even in rest from your pain,
Ye who have paid for your bliss with great sorrow:
For as it was once so it shall be again.
Ye shall cry out for death as ye stretch forth in vain

Feeble hands to the hands that would help but they may not,
Cry out to deaf ears that would hear if they could;
Till again shall the change come, and words your lips say not
Your hearts make all plain in the best wise they would
And the world ye thought waning is glorious and good:

And no morning now mocks you and no nightfall is weary,
The plains are not empty of song and of deed:
The sea strayeth not, nor the mountains are dreary;
The wind is not helpless for any man's need,
Nor falleth the rain but for thistle and weed.

O surely this morning all sorrow is hidden,
All battle is hushed for this even at least;
And no one this noontide may hunger, unbidden
To the flowers and the singing and the joy of your feast
Where silent ye sit midst the world's tale increased.

Lo, the lovers unloved that draw nigh for your blessing!
For your tale makes the dreaming whereby yet they live
The dreams of the day with their hopes of redressing,
The dreams of the night with the kisses they give,
The dreams of the dawn wherein death and hope strive.

Ah, what shall we say then, but that earth threatened often
Shall live on for ever that such things may be,
That the dry seed shall quicken, the hard earth shall soften,
And the spring-bearing birds flutter north o'er the sea,
That earth's garden may bloom round my love's feet and me?

LOVE IS ENOUGH: it grew up without heeding
　　In the days when ye knew not its name nor its measure,
　　And its leaflets untrodden by the light feet of pleasure
Had no boast of the blossom, no sign of the seeding,
　　As the morning and evening passed over its treasure.

And what do ye say then?—That Spring long departed
　　Has brought forth no child to the softness and showers;
　　−That we slept and we dreamed through the Summer of
　　flowers;
We dreamed of the Winter, and waking dead-hearted
　　Found Winter upon us and waste of dull hours.

Nay, Spring was o'er-happy and knew not the reason,
　　And Summer dreamed sadly, for she thought all was ended
　　In her fulness of wealth that might not be amended;
But this is the harvest and the garnering season,
　　And the leaf and the blossom in the ripe fruit are blended.

It sprang without sowing, it grew without heeding,
　　Ye knew not its name and ye knew not its measure,
　　Ye noted it not mid your hope and your pleasure;
There was pain in its blossom, despair in its seeding,
　　But daylong your bosom now nurseth its treasure.

CELIA LAIGHTON THAXTER
(1835–1894)

A Valentine

WHAT is the whole world worth, Dear,
    Weighed against love and truth?
Sweet is the spring to the earth, Dear,
    Bright is the blossom of youth:

And the skies of summer are tender
    In fullness of life and strength,
And rich is the autumn splendor,
    But winter comes at length.

Tell me, what spell shall charm us
    When the golden days expire?
What is there left to warm us
    Save Love's most sacred fire?

While on the soul's high altar
    Its clear light burns secure,
Though the step of joy may falter,
    And the glad years are no more,

The frosts of age are naught, Dear!
    I clasp thy hand in mine
Fondly as when youth sought, Dear,
    To be thy Valentine.

ALGERNON CHARLES SWINBURNE
(1837–1909)

The Oblation

ASK nothing more of me, sweet;
　　All I can give you I give.
　　　　Heart of my heart, were it more,
More would be laid at your feet:
　　Love that should help you to live,
　　　　Song that should spur you to soar.

All things were nothing to give
　　Once to have sense of you more,
　　　　Touch you and taste of you sweet,
Think you and breathe you and live,
　　Swept of your wings as they soar,
　　　　Trodden by chance of your feet.

I that have love and no more
　　Give you but love of you, sweet:
　　　　He that hath more, let him give;
He that hath wings, let him soar;
　　Mine is the heart at your feet
　　　　Here, that must love you to live.

A Match

IF love were what the rose is,
    And I were like the leaf,
Our lives would grow together
In sad or singing weather,
Blown fields or flowerful closes,
    Green pleasure or grey grief;
If love were what the rose is,
    And I were like the leaf.

If I were what the words are,
    And love were like the tune,
With double sound and single
Delight our lips would mingle,
With kisses glad as birds are
    That get sweet rain at noon;
If I were what the words are,
    And love were like the tune.

If you were life, my darling,
    And I your love were death,
We'd shine and snow together
Ere March made sweet the weather
With daffodil and starling
    And hours of fruitful breath;
If you were life, my darling,
    And I your love were death.

If you were thrall to sorrow,
    And I were page to joy,
We'd play for lives and seasons
With loving looks and treasons
And tears of night and morrow
    And laughs of maid and boy;
If you were thrall to sorrow,
    And I were page to joy.

If you were April's lady,
    And I were lord in May,
We'd throw with leaves for hours
And draw for days with flowers,
Till day like night were shady
    And night were bright like day;
If you were April's lady,
    And I were lord in May.

If you were queen of pleasure,
    And I were king of pain,
We'd hunt down love together,
Pluck out his flying-feather,
And teach his feet a measure,
    And find his mouth a rein;
If you were queen of pleasure,
    And I were king of pain.

Love and Sleep

LYING asleep between the strokes of night
   I saw my love lean over my sad bed,
   Pale as the duskiest lily's leaf or head,
Smooth-skinned and dark, with bare throat made to
   bite,
Too wan for blushing and too warm for white,
   But perfect-coloured without white or red.
   And her lips opened amorously, and said—
I wist not what, saving one word—Delight.
And all her face was honey to my mouth,
   And all her body pasture to mine eyes;
     The long lithe arms and hotter hands than fire,
The quivering flanks, hair smelling of the south,
     The bright light feet, the splendid supple thighs
     And glittering eyelids of my soul's desire.

MATHILDE BLIND
(1841–1896)

From: "Love in Exile"

II

WINDING all my life about thee,
   Let me lay my lips on thine;
What is all the world without thee,
    Mine —oh mine!

Let me press my heart out on thee,
   Grape of life's most fiery vine,
Spilling sacramental on thee
    Love's red wine.

Let thy strong eyes yearning o'er me
   Draw me with their force divine;
All my soul has gone before me
    Clasping thine.

Irresistibly I follow,
   As whenever we may run
Runs our shadow, as the swallow
    Seeks the sun.

Yea, I tremble, swoon, surrender
   All my spirit to thy sway,
As a star is drowned in splendour
    Of the day.

V.

I THINK of thee in watches of the night,
    I feel thee near;
Like mystic lamps consumed with too much light
    Thine eyes burn clear.

The barriers that divide us in the day
    And hide from view,
Like idle cobwebs now are brushed away
    Between us two.

I probe the deep recesses of thy mind
    Without control,
And in its inmost labyrinth I find
    My own lost soul.

No longer like an exile on the earth
    I wildly roam,
I was thy double from the hour of birth
    And thou my home.

VII.

OUR souls have touched each other,
  Two fountains from one jet;
Like children of one mother
  Our leaping thoughts have met.

We were as far asunder
  As green isles in the sea;
And now we ask in wonder
  How that could ever be.

I dare not call thee lover
  Nor any earthly name,
Though love's full cup flows over
  As water quick with flame.

When two strong minds have mated
  As only spirits may,
The wold shines new created
  In a diviner day.

Yea, though hard fate may sever
  My fleeting self from thine,
Thy thought will live for ever
  And ever grow in mine.

XXI.

I TOOK your face into my dreams,
　　It floated round me like a light;
Your beauty's consecrating beams
　　Lay mirrored in my heart all night.
As in a lonely mountain mere,
　　Unvisited of any streams,
Supremely bright and still and clear,
　　The solitary moonlight gleams,
　　Your face was shining in my dreams.

XXVI.

WHAT magic is there in thy mien
    What sorcery in thy smile,
Which charms away all cark and care,
Which turns the foul days into fair,
    And for a little while
Changes this disenchanted scene
From the sere leaf into the green,
    Transmuting with love's golden wand
    This beggared life to fairyland?

My heart goes forth to thee, oh friend,
    As some poor pilgrim to a shrine,
A pilgrim who has come from far
To seek his spirit's folding star,
    And sees the taper shine;
The goal to which his wanderings tend,
Where want and weariness shall end,
    And kneels ecstatically blest
    Because his heart hath entered rest.

L'Envoi

THOU art the goal for which my spirit longs;
    As dove on dove,
Bound for one home, I send thee all my songs
    With all my love.

Thou art the haven with fair harbour lights;
    Safe locked in thee,
My heart would anchor after stormful nights
    Alone at sea.

Thou art the rest of which my life is fain,
    The perfect peace;
Absorbed in thee the world, with all its pain
    And toil, would cease.

Thou art the heaven to which my soul would go!
    O dearest eyes,
Lost in your light you would turn hell below
    To Paradise.

Thou all in all for which my heart-blood yearns!
    Yea, near or far—
Where the unfathomed ether throbs and burns
    With star on star,

Or where, enkindled by the fires of June,
    The fresh earth glows,
Blushing beneath the mystical white moon
    Through rose on rose—

Thee, thee I see, thee feel in all live things,
    Beloved one;
In the first bird which tremulously sings
    Ere peep of sun;

In the last nestling orphaned in the hedge,
    Rocked to and fro,
When dying summer shudders in the sedge,
    And swallows go;

When roaring snows rush down the mountain-pass,
    March floods with rills
Or April lightens through the living grass
    In daffodils;

When poppied cornfields simmer in the heat
    With tare and thistle,
And, like winged clouds above the mellow wheat,
    The starlings whistle;

When stained with sunset the wide moorlands glare
    In the wild weather,
And clouds with flaming craters smoke and flare
    Red o'er red heather;

When the bent moon, on frostbound midnights
    waking,
    Leans to the snow
Like some world-mother whose deep heart is breaking
    O'er human woe.

As the round sun rolls red into the ocean,
    Till all the sea
Glows fluid gold, even so life's mazy motion
    Is dyed with thee:

For as the wave-like years subside and roll,
    O heart's desire,
Thy soul glows interfused within my soul,
    A quenchless fire.

Yea, thee I feel, all storms of life above,
    Near though afar;
O thou my glorious morning star of love,
    And evening star.

EDWARD ROWLAND SILL
(1841–1887)

To a Maid Demure

OFTEN when the night is come,
With its quiet group at home,
While they broider, knit, or sew,
Read, or chat in voices low,
Suddenly you lift your eyes
With an earnest look, and wise;
But I cannot read their lore,—
Tell me less, or tell me more.

Like a picture in a book,
Pure and peaceful is your look,
Quietly you walk your ways;
Steadfast duty fills the days.
Neither tears nor fierce delights,
Feverish days nor tossing nights,
Any troublous dreams confess,—
Tell me more, or tell me less.

Swift the weeks are on the wing;
Years are brief, and love a thing
Blooming, fading, like a flower;
Wake and seize the little hour.
Give me welcome, or farewell;
Quick! I wait! And who can tell
What to-morrow may befall,—
Love me more, or not at all.

The Lover's Song

LEND me thy fillet, Love!
    I would no longer see;
Cover mine eyelids close awhile,
    And make me blind like thee.

Then might I pass her sunny face,
    And know not it was fair;
Then might I hear her voice, nor guess
    Her starry eyes were there.

Ah! banished so from stars and sun—
    Why need it be my fate?
If only she might dream me good
    And wise, and be my mate!

Lend her thy fillet, Love!
    Let her no longer see:
If there is hope for me at all,
    She must be blind like thee.

ALFRED JOYCE KILMER
(1886–1918)

A Valentine

My songs should be as lilies fair,
    And roses made of crimson light,
To lie amid the fragrant hair
    And on the breast of my delight.

Such glory is for them too high;
    I'll scatter them adown the street,
And when my love is passing by
    They will rise up and kiss her feet.